Paraprofessionals and Teachers Working Together

Highly Effective Strategies for Inclusive Classrooms

Third Edition

DEDICATION

To Norma Sanchez, Kathy Wicker, Ginger Davis, Bethany Moody, Yvette Kazynski, and Mary Ellen McGrath; outstanding paraprofessionals who I was blessed to work with over the years.

Paraprofessionals and Teachers Working Together

Highly Effective Strategies for Inclusive Classrooms

Third Edition

Susan Gingras Fitzell, M.Ed.

Cogent Catalyst Publications

Paraprofessionals and Teachers Working Together

Copyright © 2017 by Susan Gingras Fitzell

Printed in the United States of America.

Library of Congress Cataloging-in-Publication Data
        Fitzell, Susan Gingras
        Includes bibliographic references
        ISBN 978-1-932995-37-4 (pbk.)
        1. Teaching Teams 2. Classroom Management

Paraprofessionals and Teachers Working Together
Highly Effective Strategies for Inclusive Classrooms

If you have questions or would like customized school in-service or ongoing consultation, contact:

Susan Gingras Fitzell
PO Box 6182
Manchester, NH 03108-6182
603-625-6087 or 210-473-2863
sfitzell@susanfitzell.com
www.susanfitzell.com

GET YOUR BONUS RESOURCES HERE:
http://Bonus374.susanfitzell.com

ABOUT THE AUTHOR

Susan Gingras Fitzell, M.Ed., CSP, has been consulting, writing, and presenting since 1993 and has spent over 15 years onsite in organizations throughout the United States working hand- in-hand with teachers, management, and employees helping them to increase productivity, learning, and problem-solving to reach their goals.

She has authored over a dozen books and is one of only 650 certified speaking professionals in the world today. Susan is a dynamic, nationally recognized speaker as well as an innovative change agent, compassionate coach, and effective productivity & learning expert. After working with Susan, clients are more efficient, productive, and effective.

She is a black belt in kickboxing and a student of kung fu. Her family prides themselves in being geeks and her two adult children have both earned degrees in mechanical engineering using the strategies that Susan shares with her clients.

Other selected titles by Susan Gingras Fitzell, M.Ed.:
- 100+ Tech Ideas for Teaching English and Language Arts
- Special Needs in the General Classroom: 500+ Teaching Strategies for Differentiating Instruction, 3rd Edition
- Co-Teaching and Collaboration in the Classroom: Strategies for Success
- Free the Children: Conflict Education for Strong & Peaceful Minds
- Memorization and Test-Taking Strategies
- Motivating Students to Choose Success
- Please Help Me with My Homework! Strategies for Parents and Caregivers (English and Spanish)
- RTI Strategies for Secondary Teachers
- Transforming Anger to Personal Power: An Anger Management Curriculum for Grades 6 through 12
- Umm Studying? What's That? Learning Strategies for the Overwhelmed and Confused College and High School Student
- Use iPads and Other Cutting-Edge Technology to Strengthen Your Instruction

TABLE OF CONTENTS

ℬ CHAPTER 5 ℚ

FOSTERING STUDENT INDEPENDENCE

ℬCONCLUSIONℚ

READ FIRST

This book is designed to help you meet the challenges that occur when paraprofessionals and teachers work together in an inclusive classroom. You will find techniques for collaboration between paraprofessionals and classroom teachers and specialists.

Whereas the book was intended for both teachers and paraprofessionals to benefit, each section considers the level of authority that paraprofessionals do and don't have. For example, the behavior management and academic strategy chapters primarily include strategies that can be implemented by a paraprofessional without conflicting with a teacher's assignments or discipline style.

The strategies and approaches include practical, proven ways to differentiate academic assignments and expectations as well as materials to increase the effectiveness of instruction and meet Individual Education Plan (IEP) adaptations in the general classroom without reducing content.

These approaches and techniques work for ALL youth in the inclusive classroom and are critical for students with special needs.

Definitions

Teach: For the purpose of this book, teach is being used generically, without requirement of a teaching certification. It is used the same context as we might say parents teach, counselors teach, coaches teach. Clearly, to design instruction, an educator needs a teaching certificate. Paraprofessionals teach under the supervision of a certified teacher.

Paraprofessional: Para is a prefix that in Greek means, "at or to one side of, beside, side by side." I prefer this term as well as paraeducator because it is, to me, a respectful title. The paraprofessional stands beside the professional. The paraprofessional is not less than the professional.

A motto that works:
GOOD FOR ALL, CRITICAL FOR DIFFERENT LEARNERS!

❧ CHAPTER 1 ❧

Build a Strong Foundation for Success

The Two Most Important Things

One of the most important aspects of an effective working relationship between the paraprofessional, special educator, teacher, or specialist is clear and consistent communication and organization. It is critical to communicate frequently and use organizational structures and tools that can help define roles, define expectations, and set parameters for class norms as part of the communication process.

On a more tangible level, it's critical to organize the paraprofessional's schedule in a way that is efficient, practical, and mindful of everyone's needs and job requirements. So often, paraprofessionals are scheduled into classrooms at the last minute allowing no time for the teacher and paraprofessional to build a solid foundation based on communication and understanding before attempting to work together.

Why is structure and time to communicate so important? Because without having a system in place to discuss issues, organize information, and handle variables, much is subject to guesswork, and guesswork often causes problems and communication breakdown.

A paraprofessional[1] often enters the classroom with a tremendous amount of concern about intruding on the teacher's space. Many times, this concern can lead to inaction, a lesser quality of experience for both the paraeducator and teacher, and sometimes can even lead to feelings of intimidation. Time spent communicating - establishing rapport, documenting, and organizing roles, expectations, and schedules - can make the difference between a harmonious relationship and one filled with discord.

It is important for both teachers and paraeducators to understand that a paraprofessional's job is demanding and varies tremendously from one class to another. He may not know what he will encounter in any one situation, what he will be required to do once he walks in that classroom door, or what personalities he may have to navigate.

One of the trickiest parts of working in the classroom as a paraprofessional is understanding the paraprofessional's role. What is that role? Each

---

[1] Paraprofessional, paraeducator, teacher assistant, teacher aide, etc. are used interchangeably in education. This text will use paraprofessional and paraeducator to refer to this job title.

student's needs determine the paraprofessional's role, whether they are academic needs or behavioral needs, and often these are dictated by the IEP or the special education department.

Sometimes a paraprofessional is working with one single student. Other times, a paraprofessional may be working with an entire class of students. In that situation, the paraprofessional may be working as a classroom assistant because many students in the classroom are on an IEP.

It is very difficult in these situations to walk into a classroom without any prior dialogue as to what the paraprofessional's roles and responsibilities will include. The paraprofessional's job is to support and assist students within the classroom using the IEPs of the student, or several students, involved to provide the framework. The supervising special or general education teacher is responsible for direct instruction, providing assistance, and guiding the paraprofessional to work effectively with individual students. It is important that the paraprofessional feels positive about the work he or she is doing and feels in harmony with the classroom teacher.(Giangreco, Edelman, & Broer, 2001)

The Paraprofessionals' Role

A Paraprofessional's Point of View

Dear Teacher,

Teamwork between the paraprofessional and the classroom teacher is an essential ingredient to a successful inclusion classroom. When a paraprofessional is assigned to a class, he or she should be seen as a part of the solution and not as an intrusion.

Ideally, the paraprofessional and the classroom teacher have some common planning time to discuss upcoming assignments, progress of students, and methods to help the students succeed. Without this time, it is difficult to establish a strong working relationship; however, the relationship can still be beneficial.

Paraprofessionals can be valuable resources in the classroom. They can work in class with students who are having difficulty understanding the information, provide notes for those students who are unable to take comprehensive notes during class time, and provide help with test and assignment modifications for students with learning disabilities.

Student follow-up is especially important to meet IEP requirements and promote success. Often, the paraprofessional can follow-up in the resource room as well as in class. Paraprofessionals can support the classroom teacher by answering the questions of all students.

Paraprofessionals are an integral and important part of the classroom team. They are happy to contribute whatever they can to add to the success of all the students. If the teacher is accepting of the paraprofessional's presence, then the students will also accept it as normal and will consider him or her as the extra, valuable resource he or she is.

Ginger Davis
Londonderry High School

Defining the Role of the Paraprofessional

Least Effective Use of Paraeducators' Skills(Brock & Carter, 2013; McVay, 1998):

The general education teacher and students both lose a valuable resource if the paraprofessional's role is to:
- Photocopy papers
- Copy notes (solely)
- Run errands
- Hold up the back wall of the classroom, figuratively speaking.

Ways Paraprofessionals Support Inclusive Classrooms

The ways a paraprofessional might assist in the classroom are as individual as the students they are responsible for, the classrooms they work in, and the grade level they teach.

On the following pages are checklists filled with options for the general education teacher, the special education teacher, and the paraprofessional to consider when defining paraprofessional roles in the classroom.

Use these checklists as tools to negotiate the working relationship in the classroom before the paraprofessional starts "on the job."

One-to-One Assistant

Classroom Teacher:
Subject:
Student Initials:

- ☐ Support student in getting ready for in-class assignments or for other activities so he or she can keep up with the class while at the same time learning how to become more independent.
- ☐ Substitute activities without changing curriculum.
- ☐ Adapt instructional materials in accordance with the IEP.
- ☐ Re-teach instruction and provide reinforcement.
- ☐ Assist the student with individual activities.
- ☐ Assist student with interpreting and following directions.
- ☐ Modify assignments as directed by the special education teacher or the general education teacher.
- ☐ Administer tests individually reinforcing skills that the teacher previously taught.
- ☐ Read aloud to the students.
- ☐ Assist with organizational skills.
- ☐ Create educational memory games and activities.
- ☐ Keep records to document behavior of individual students.
- ☐ Maintain a daily journal or log communicating with parents or other classroom teachers regarding class work, homework, or daily activities.
- ☐ Facilitate social opportunities and interactions for all students.
- ☐ Supervise student who might leave the classroom for a break or might leave to go to another classroom.
- ☐ Check for work completion and homework.
- ☐ Copy notes occasionally or assist with note-taking.
- ☐ Support student when involved with group work.
- ☐ Cue/refocus/redirect student.
- ☐ Create review worksheets.
- ☐ Assist with the testing process.
- ☐ Use Boardmaker® by Mayer-Johnson[2] or find clipart pictures to assist student's ability to communicate.
- ☐ Create a "find and point" communication tool for the student.
- ☐ Help create "social stories" for student (autistic spectrum).
- ☐ Create a picture schedule list, color-coded, and teach the student to be as independent as possible with this schedule.

---

[2] http://www.mayer-johnson.com/boardmaker-software

Small Group Assistance

Classroom Teacher:
Subject:

- ☐ Substitute activities without changing curriculum.
- ☐ Adapt instructional materials in accordance with the IEP.
- ☐ Provide remedial instruction and reinforcement skills.
- ☐ Assist the students with individual activities.
- ☐ Help students with makeup work.
- ☐ Assist students with interpreting and following directions.
- ☐ Make on-the-spot adaptations to curriculum and instruction according to pre-established guidelines.
- ☐ Assist with organizational skills.
- ☐ Check for work completion or homework.
- ☐ Create educational memory games and activities.
- ☐ Conduct learning activities as directed by the classroom teacher.
- ☐ Facilitate social opportunities and interactions.
- ☐ Support students involved with group work.
- ☐ Cue, refocus, or redirect students.
- ☐ Read aloud to students.
- ☐ Review for tests.
- ☐ _____.
- ☐ _____.
- ☐ _____.
- ☐ _____.
- ☐ _____.
- ☐ _____.
- ☐ _____.
- ☐ _____.

Social/Behavioral Assistance

Classroom Teacher:
Subject:
Student Initials:

Behavioral Assistance
- ☐ Cue, refocus, or redirect students.
- ☐ Implement position control (positioning oneself in the classroom as a behavior management strategy).
- ☐ Help create "social stories" for students in the autistic spectrum.
- ☐ Assist with classroom management by implementing class rules.
- ☐ Keep records to document behavior of individual students.
- ☐ Supervise students who might leave the classroom for break or might leave to go to another classroom.
- ☐ Supervise individual students or groups of students at various times of day, such as lunch, recess, or when the teacher is out of the room.
- ☐ Supervise students during lunch, recess, assemblies, or when getting on or off the bus.
- ☐ _____.
- ☐ _____.
- ☐ _____.

Social Assistance
- ☐ Create a picture schedule list, color-coded, and teach the student to be as independent as possible with this schedule.
- ☐ Enlist peers to help a student gather and carry materials.
- ☐ Facilitate social opportunities and interactions for all students.

- ☐ _____.
- ☐ _____.
- ☐ _____.
- ☐ _____.

Academic Assistance

Classroom Teacher:
Subject:
Student Initials:

- ☐ Support student in getting ready for in-class assignments or other activities so he or she can keep up with the class while, at the same time, learning how to become more independent.
- ☐ Monitor the student's level of participation in the classroom.
- ☐ Help the classroom teacher with instructional strategies or other supports that are required in the IEP.
- ☐ Adapt instructional materials in accordance with the IEP.
- ☐ Provide remedial instruction and reinforcement skills.
- ☐ Assist students with individual activities.
- ☐ Help students with makeup work.
- ☐ Assist students with interpreting and following directions.
- ☐ Modify assignments for specific students as directed by the special education teacher or the general education teacher.
- ☐ Administer tests individually.
- ☐ Reinforce skills that the teacher previously taught.
- ☐ Read aloud to the students.
- ☐ Assist with organizational skills.
- ☐ Check for work completion or homework.
- ☐ Conduct learning activities as directed by the classroom teacher for a small group of students.
- ☐ Maintain a daily journal or log communicating with parents or other classroom teachers regarding class work, homework, or daily activities.
- ☐ Copy notes occasionally or assist with note-taking.
- ☐ Support students involved with group work.
- ☐ Assist with the testing process.
- ☐ Follow-up with the student outside the classroom.
- ☐ Motivate and support students with homework.
- ☐ Work with drop-in center, learning center, or resource room to help students focus and stay on track.
- ☐ Ask questions in class.
- ☐ Answer questions in class.
- ☐ Review for tests with small groups of students.
- ☐ Guide student-centered activities.
- ☐ Serve as a scribe.

Physical Assistance

Classroom Teacher:
Subject:
Student Initials:

- ☐ Serve as a personal care attendant when appropriate.
- ☐ Assist with personal hygiene, including feeding and diapering.
- ☐ Assist students with motor or mobility limitations.
- ☐ Assist students with individual activities.
- ☐ Maintain a daily journal or log communicating with parents or other classroom teachers regarding class work, homework, or daily activities.
- ☐ Supervise students who might leave the classroom for break or might leave to go to another classroom.
- ☐ Supervise individual students or groups of students at various times of day, such as at lunch, recess, or when the teacher is out of the room.
- ☐ Supervise students during lunch, recess, assemblies, or when getting on or off the bus. Use Boardmaker® by Mayer-Johnson[3] or find clipart pictures to assist student's ability to communicate.
- ☐ Create a "find and point" communication tool for the student.
- ☐ Serve as a scribe.
- ☐ _____.
- ☐ _____.
- ☐ _____.
- ☐ _____.
- ☐ _____.
- ☐ _____.
- ☐ _____.
- ☐ _____.

---

[3] http://www.mayer-johnson.com/boardmaker-software

Teacher Support

(Not Hired Specifically for Special Education Needs)
Classroom Teacher:
Subject:

- ☐ Help the classroom teacher with instructional strategies or other supports that are required in the IEP.
- ☐ Conduct learning activities as directed by the classroom teacher for a small group of students.
- ☐ Make instructional materials for the whole class so that the teacher can work with individual students.
- ☐ Supervise individual students or groups of students at various times of day, such as at lunch, recess, or when the teacher is out of the room.
- ☐ Supervise students during lunch, recess, assemblies, or when getting on or off the bus.
- ☐ Make copies of notes.
- ☐ Create review worksheets.
- ☐ Assist with the testing process.
- ☐ Answer questions in class.
- ☐ Implement position control (positioning oneself in the classroom as a behavior management strategy).
- ☐ Guide student-centered activities.
- ☐ Assist with classroom management by implementing classroom rules.

- ☐ _____.
- ☐ _____.
- ☐ _____.
- ☐ _____.
- ☐ _____.
- ☐ _____.
- ☐ _____.

Differentiating Roles - A Legal Priority

What is the teacher's role? What is the paraprofessional's role? It is critical that the supervising teacher, the paraprofessional and, when appropriate, the special educator clearly define classroom roles. Some responsibilities should not be assigned to paraprofessionals. Tasks that could pose legal or safety threats to the paraprofessional, that violate union rules, or tasks that are not appropriate or fair are examples of such responsibilities.

Should a paraprofessional be left alone in the classroom? This dilemma challenges most schools and districts given the shortage of substitute teachers. There have been times when I have had a paraprofessional in the classroom and I needed to slip out for a valid reason and the paraprofessional covered my class. This, however, is rarely part of a paraprofessional's job description. Regardless, it sometimes happens in the real world. It is important to be aware and knowledgeable of the paraprofessional's role and to make sure paraprofessionals are not put in positions where they might be liable for more than what is legally or contractually appropriate. The paraprofessional should not be responsible for the classroom if the supervising teacher is absent.

Because paraprofessionals were often more knowledgeable and better equipped to manage the class in my absence, when I needed to be out for a day, a substitute teacher would often follow my paraprofessional's lead. The district eventually "hired" paraprofessionals as the substitute teacher with the pay and protections one gets with that job. The paraprofessional was under a substitute contract for a day. This option might work in some schools; however, it is important that this option be exercised within the rules of the state and within the guidelines for the district.

In addition, the paraprofessional should never be responsible for designing curriculum or modifying content. For example, a reduction of content is not appropriate unless the paraprofessional has been authorized to make that modification based on IEP requirements and the recommendation of the general educator and the special education teacher. Paraprofessionals are not responsible for creating lesson plans or providing initial instruction for students.

Paraprofessionals may provide additional reinforcement, may create adaptations and activities that enhance learning, memory, and recall.

The chart on the next page, provided by the Kansas Department of Education clarifies the difference between the teachers' role and the paraprofessionals role.

The teacher and paraprofessional represent a differentiated team. The following comparison highlights the differences in the roles of the teacher and the paraprofessional in various aspects of the program.

Classroom Organization

Teacher Role	Paraprofessional Role
Plans weekly schedule, lessons, room arrangements, learning centers, and activities for individuals and the entire class.	Implements plan as specified by the teacher.

Assessment

Teacher Role	Paraprofessional Role
Administers and scores formal and informal tests.	Administers informal tests.

Setting Objectives

Teacher Role	Paraprofessional Role
Determines appropriate objectives for groups and individual children.	Carries out activities to meet objectives.

Teaching

Teacher Role	Paraprofessional Role
Teaches lessons for the entire class, small groups, and individual children.	Reinforces and supervises practice of skills with individual and small groups.

Behavior Management

Teacher Role	Paraprofessional Role
Observes behavior, plans and implements behavior management strategies for entire class and for individual children.	Observes behavior, carries out behavior management activities.

Working with Parents

Teacher Role	Paraprofessional Role
Meets with parents and initiates conferences concerning child's progress.	Participates in parent conferences when appropriate.

Building a Classroom Partnership

Teacher Role	Paraprofessional Role
Arranges schedule for conferences, shares goals and philosophy with paraprofessional, organizes job duties for paraprofessional.	Shares ideas and concerns during conferences and carries out duties as directed by a teacher.

[4]

---

[4] *Guidelines for the Training, Utilization, and Supervision of Paraprofessionals and Aides* Published by the Kansas State Department of Education, Topeka, Kansas

Communicating to Set Clear Expectations

To have a more harmonious and effective working relationship in the classroom, it is important to be on the same page with matters of concern in the classroom. Consider discussing how the paraprofessional will plan for his or her work in the classroom. Other items to consider include "How will the paraprofessional meet instructional goals? What are the teacher's expectations for participation in classroom management? How will the classroom teacher and paraprofessional communicate with each other?"

Para/Teacher Communication Starter Form

Lesson Planning

- Will the paraprofessional provide input into the planning process for either specific students or the class in general? If so, how will the classroom teacher gain that input?

- Will the paraprofessional have input into lesson planning or planning for re-teaching? How and when will that input be communicated?

- When and how should the paraprofessional's experience in the classroom contribute to interventions used with non-responders or students with special needs?

Instruction

- With whom will the paraprofessional work: students with special needs, non-responders, students at risk, or the general student population?

- Will the paraprofessional re-teach material? ___ Yes ___ No

- When and how will the need for re-teaching be decided?

- How will the paraprofessional help implement lesson plans or provide re-teaching? What will this look like?

- If specific interventions or programs are being utilized, who will train the paraprofessional in these methods?

- When will student assessment take place? How will gains be recorded? Who will be responsible for collecting this data?

Student Behavior

- What are the behavioral expectations and rules for students in the classroom? (Attach guidelines)

- What methods are used to gain student understanding of classroom expectations and rules?

How do we want the students to perceive those expectations and rules in regard to the paraprofessional's authority? Who clarifies the paraprofessional's level of authority? How will the teacher support the paraprofessional's authority in the classroom?

- How should the paraprofessional deal with misbehavior, disruptions, or problems that occur in the classroom?

- Who will provide the paraprofessional with positive behavior management training when necessary?

Communication

- How and when will professionals and paraprofessionals communicate about concerns, student updates, intervention progress, etc.?

- Who will be responsible for communicating with parents?

- Will communication with parents be verbal or written? What parameters should the paraprofessional work within?

- When should communication be deferred to the classroom teacher, special educator, or administrator?

- When should conversations with parents be documented? When should they not be documented?

- If documented, what form should that documentation take?

- Exactly who should the paraprofessional report to if any conversation with a parent occurs that might cause concerns, or where student issues need to be related?

Tips for Success: Paraprofessionals

Behavior Management
- Explain and help small groups set the ground rules so student interaction is positive and productive.
- Ensure that students own their behavior by using strategies and language that takes the responsibility off you and keeps it where it belongs — on the child.

Foster Relationships
- Encourage students to make friendships in the classroom so they feel empowered and learn to be more independent.
- Position yourself so that the teacher communicates directly with the student, enabling them to develop a rapport.
- Encourage other students to interact with students with special needs.

Provide Support so that All Benefit
- Ask questions. It is helpful to the teacher and to other students in class. Feel free to offer suggestions. At times, you may want to offer them to the teacher privately; however, offering suggestions appropriately in the classroom is a wonderful advantage to the class as a whole.
- Consider yourself a helper to all students in the classroom. This benefits the teacher, reduces stigma on the student with special needs, and supports all students in the room.
- Move around the room. At times, it will be necessary and critical to be near your assigned student(s). However, it is just as critical for student(s) to be on their own to develop independence.
- Ask yourself, "How would I feel if I had an adult right next to me all day long?" Have the courage to give students personal space to interact with the classroom teacher, other students, and to work independently.

Don't try to be a Lone Ranger
- Get help when you need it. Everyone needs help at times.
- When you must make quick, on-the-spot decisions or adaptations while providing instructions, it is critical to discuss these decisions with

the general and/or special education teacher as soon as possible so they can provide necessary feedback.

Foster Independence

- Allow and encourage students to do anything and everything they can and should do for themselves. If we fall into the trap of doing too much for the child, we encourage learned helplessness.
- Try to remember that no matter what the cognitive age of the child, it is important to treat him or her socially in accordance with his or her chronological age. The more we expect, the more they will deliver, within reason.
- Expect and encourage age-appropriate social behavior.

Maintain Confidentiality

- Avoid discussing your students with others outside the classroom unless they also work with the student and have a legal right to that information.
- If you are unsure about what can be shared without violating confidentiality, defer, and refer to the teacher or your supervisor.
- Don't identify students you work with to others when you see them out in the community. Be careful in social situations of providing too much information (TMI).
- Keep what you say and write about a student positive! Use initials instead of full names where appropriate.

Empower your Teacher

- Be flexible. Sometimes your ability to be flexible provides a huge service to your collaborating teacher. The classroom can be an unpredictable place and the more we are able to roll with the changes, the better it will be for everyone.
- Sometimes, you'll be working with a new teacher. It's possible you have many years of experience and have set ideas on what works and what doesn't. Empower your teacher. Make suggestions, and respect his/her choices. Try not to take offense if your experience is ignored. Every teacher needs to find their own way. They need your support in the process.

Be Amazing

- Identify and rally your strengths. You have expertise that benefits the child and the teacher in the classroom. Use it.

Teachers

Empower your Paraprofessional

- Consider the paraprofessional an essential member of your teaching team. Whenever possible, include the paraprofessional in planning, team meetings, troubleshooting, and any other decision where you feel input from the paraprofessional may be valuable. Paraprofessionals in my world are just as human as I am. I always treated my paraprofessionals with respect and as equals, and that always enhanced my relationships and the effectiveness of the paraprofessionals in my classroom.

Behavior Management

- Empower the paraprofessional to monitor behavior and support the discipline process in the classroom. This empowerment will be worth millions when you must leave the classroom with a substitute, knowing that you have challenging students in the room. You will be able to rest more comfortably knowing that the paraprofessional can handle the class and that students will respect that person's authority.
- Teach the paraprofessional how to handle discipline issues in your classroom.

Communicate, Communicate, Communicate

- Discuss your goals, your priorities, and plans with your paraprofessionals daily. Sometimes this may mean stealing a few minutes of time before class, while students are doing a quiet seat activity, or after class. Communication is critical, not only to the success of students in the classroom, but also to the teaching relationship.
- Discuss issues with your paraprofessional, especially when the issue is related to the student he or she is working with. Oftentimes, a paraprofessional has an outside view that we as teachers tend to miss. Their ideas and possible solutions could be invaluable in a difficult situation.

- Inform your paraprofessional of critical information regarding students he or she is involved with or information that could affect classroom dynamics. Ask the paraprofessional what he or she needs to know to do the job most effectively.

Provide Visuals, Notes, and Models

- Take notes of your procedures, preferences, and lesson nuances and document those notes on easy-to-remember or easy-to-use forms so that they can be referred to throughout the year. This is critical for paraprofessionals who are working with more than one teacher because each teacher may have different expectations.
- Compile a loose-leaf binder for the paraprofessional that contains class rules, expectations, a syllabus, etc.
- Model how you want things done. For example, model for the paraprofessional how to administer tests.
- Model the difference between "cueing" a student to remember an answer vs. giving the student the answer.
- Model/teach how to respond to specific behavior.
- Provide scripts when necessary to assist the paraprofessional in responding to student behavior.

Be Proactive

- Have a welcome interview with your team. For example, a team might include a special educator, the general educator, and a paraprofessional. Learn more about one another and develop an initial understanding of your roles and responsibilities.
- Provide the paraprofessional with lesson plans, activities, or "to do" items as soon as possible. Last minute rushes often stress the paraprofessional and do not allow for proper preparation time.

Nurture and Protect your Relationship

- Avoid interruption when the paraeducator is working with a student or several students. Interruption undermines the paraprofessional's authority with the students, and often causes distress and possible conflict.
- Provide very specific, positive feedback so they know what they are doing right and feel appreciated.

Delegating Tasks to Paraprofessionals

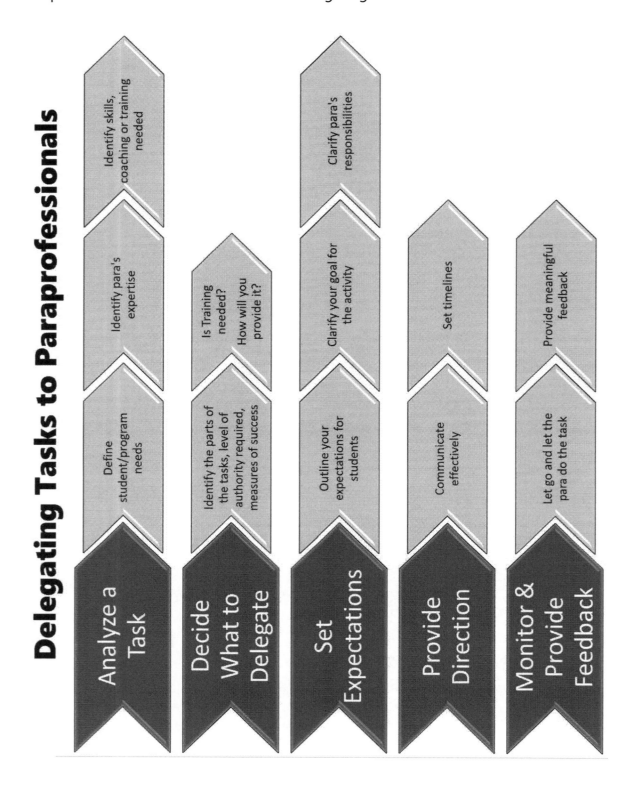

Analyze a Task
- Define student/program needs
- Identify para's expertise
- Identify skills, coaching or training needed

Decide What to Delegate
- Identify the parts of the tasks, level of authority required, measures of success
- Is Training needed? How will you provide it?

Set Expectations
- Outline your expectations for students
- Clarify your goal for the activity
- Clarify para's responsibilities

Provide Direction
- Communicate effectively
- Set timelines

Monitor & Provide Feedback
- Let go and let the para do the task
- Provide meaningful feedback

[5] *Guidelines for the Training, Utilization, and Supervision of Paraprofessionals and Aides* Published by the Kansas State Department of Education, Topeka, Kansas

Collecting and Sharing Data

Ways to Collect Data

- Have students self-assess.
- Keep a notebook or journal to track objective observations and observations. Stick to the *facts*. Opinions are best left unwritten.
- Customize a form that suits each individual situation or student to track information easily.
- Keep a portfolio of student work or samples to display how the student is progressing.

Data Collection Considerations

Consider the following core questions regarding what data to collect:

- What is the goal of collecting this information? For example, is the goal to document behavior? To monitor progress towards IEP goals and objectives? To determine which adaptations or modifications work best? Or to determine what may or may not be working?
- What types of information do I need to collect to reach the goal? What is the function of the student's behavior? What do you think the student is getting out of his or her behavior? What is the "antecedent" to the student's behavior? (Information about the student's activities, social skills, physical needs, and emotional well-being, etc. is good to include.)
- Am I responsible for summarizing the data and writing the report?
- When should I be gathering this information? How often? Under what conditions?
- How will this information be used? Where will this information be used, and under what circumstances will it be used? Will it be used in an IEP meeting? Will it be for the parents' benefit? Will it be used by the classroom teacher? The special educator? The administrator?
- Who may see this information? (Consult with the Special Education supervisor to find out who will be able to access this information.)
- Make sure that the information collected adheres to confidentiality laws, respects the student's and parents' sensitivities, and does not hurt or hinder the education or progress of the student.
- If data being collected makes you uncomfortable, it is important to address this issue with your supervisor. Do not do anything you are

uncomfortable with without analyzing the reasons for your discomfort and making an informed decision on how to move forward. Listen to the red flags that go up in your mind and in your heart.

- For your safety and the legal safety of the school, stick to the *FACTS.* Avoid writing down your opinions, feelings, conclusions, theories, etc. Save those things for when the time is appropriate to discuss them. Be careful about what you put on paper. Paper can be subpoenaed.

- Be *very* careful what you write in email or say on a voice mail. Be careful when sharing information from the Internet. If written on a school computer, it is archived and can be undeleted. Voicemail can be forwarded. This information can be subpoenaed.

Things That Can Get Educators in Legal Hot Water![6]

Remember those World War II posters that warned, "Loose Lips Sink Ships?" Well, that dire wisdom is just as urgent today. It is possible that a comment ingenuously made in the faculty room, in an email, during an IEP meeting or a phone call can cause an educator embarrassment, at best, or a district to become embroiled in a lawsuit, at worst. Caution for being professional always, as well as ever mindful of confidentiality laws, has always been a top priority of school districts. However, in our digital age, this issue has taken on a new meaning and has escalated caution to another level.

To ferret out the most critical concerns facing schools today and some tips for how to deal with these concerns, I spoke with four lawyers who work with schools on a regular basis. Following are some of the insights gleaned from those conversations.

What Is Considered Written Documentation?

Anything and everything written about a student on school grounds can be subpoenaed for use in court. Attorney Dianna Halpenny of Sacramento, California, reinforces that anything in writing with a student's name in it is part of the official student record. It is not necessarily true that if educators keep it at home that it is not a student record.

---

[6] Copyright © 2010, Susan Fitzell & Aim Hi Educational Programs, LLC. First published April 28, 2010. Adapted to apply to all educators – teachers and paraprofessionals.

Email Communication

When faced with the challenge of keeping email private on school servers, educators used to be advised to use web mail versus a downloadable email client such as Microsoft Outlook, Eudora, or Thunderbird. The belief was that web mail such as Yahoo mail, Hotmail, Mail2Web, etc. were safe.

Attorney Pamela Parker of Austin, Texas, reveals another, less known, fact: even web-based email is forensically accessible. Web-based email history may still be on the school server. Parker acknowledges that schools are not necessarily monitoring emails; however, a forensic computer specialist can recreate the emails if necessary. The reality of today's world is that everything that is digital lives forever. Parker employs a sound analogy, "Having a conversation by email or text message is no different than having a private conversation on stage at Carnegie hall in front of a full house. Most people won't pay attention, but some will."

Educators may send an email to a parent, colleague, supervisor, etc. believing that the email will remain confidential between them. However, there is no guarantee that the recipient of an email will respect that confidentiality or realize the importance of keeping the interaction private. Sometimes, despite all good intentions, emails are forwarded accidentally. This easily happens when the writer uses "reply all" or continues to respond to an email that has the entire thread attached. I've been amazed at what I've had included in a message to me when I have been added as a recipient midstream in an email conversation. When I scroll down, I might read conversation to which I should not have been privy. Here's a tip: Look at what's attached to the bottom of your email before you hit "send!"

Phone Messages

Another consideration is phone messages. Not only can they be overheard, they can be forwarded. Parker contends that even an educator's children might see and pass on text messages or phone emails. Parker advises educators to have critical conversations in person.

Attorney Brad King of Richmond, Virginia, goes on to explain that even messages on personal phones, especially those regarding relationships with students, can become public domain. He explains that educators' phone records can be involved in litigation. Again, the digital age brings a new level of accountability to the issue. Digital phone messages, as well as text messages, are easily forwarded and potentially retrieved.

Text Messages

Have you ever gotten a text or sent a text that was meant for someone else? Are you sure that deleted texts are not potentially accessible if a related case was brought to court? How much text messaging is available is dependent on your telecommunication carrier. There may be information out there that you do not know is there.

What About Verbal Conversation?

In School
King stresses that educators might vent in the faculty room, hall, or office believing that they are in safe territory and in trustworthy company. They might comment while scheduling an IEP meeting, "Oh, this is that 'high maintenance parent.'" If that comment is overheard and related back to that parent through the grapevine, it might cause the parent to be inflamed, at the least.

At Home
Educators frequently talk about personal information when venting and it can, and often does, come back to haunt them. If educators need to vent, vent at home without mentioning specifics about, or identifying, the student with whom they are having issues.

In the Community
Halpenny adds that it's important to be aware of surroundings outside of school, too. For example, an educator's conversation with a friend in the grocery store may easily be overheard.

Consequences of Venting

In some cases, it's natural for educators to vent frustration over behavior by students or parents that feels unjust, provocative, and problematic. However, if educators express that frustration in writing, without reserve, using language that is perceived as derogatory, profane, or slanderous they are at risk of that written documentation being discovered and forwarded to unintended recipients.

Attorney Mark Joel Goldstein, Milwaukee, WI, reiterates that in a faculty room, conversation can be a matter of perception in the moment (complimented by tone of voice and body language). However, in the digital age, there may be a record of it and, without any accompanying tone of voice or body language, that record can be more easily misinterpreted or misportrayed. The consequence might be as light as a reprimand and embarrassment or as dire as job dismissal. As King explains, it's considered disrespectful to the people that educators are supposed to serve when that educator berates or publicly criticizes those very people.

Another common area of trouble for educators is when they vent online regarding an issue that they feel is unjust towards them, thereby circumventing due process and appropriate hierarchical chains of command. Goldstein explains there is a grievance process framed by set lines of authority and a clear hierarchy. The process gets undermined when you use digital information. When educators broadcast their vent online, the proper protocol is undermined. It's possible that the very people that are in a position to help will not be able to support the educator because the issue has been muddied by emotional statements posted online.

Protocol for Necessary Conversations

Do these recommendations only apply to situations where educators might be tempted to vent? Not according to Parker. She emphasizes that educators should not talk about disciplinary issues, educational matters, or medical information with people who are not directly related to providing services to that student. Parker explains that sometimes this 'chat' is innocent; however, in those informal chats educators will be less conscious about talking about the issue in a professional way. If they are discussing these things with someone who is not involved in providing service, that person may not be as conscious of confidentiality and may pass the information around.

Educator-Student Relationships

Even when an educator's intentions are good, they can find themselves in hot water. Halpenny adds that when educators try to be a friend to students who have emotional problems it can backfire. This presents a situation as precarious as when an educator starts engaging a student too much outside of school.

There was a time when educators were free to give a student a ride home in their car, take students out for lunch, or to play pool after school to build relationships, or even make home visits. Those times have essentially passed. Educators put themselves at risk if they interact with students outside of school boundaries. When I was in high school, my speech coach took me and another male student to the beach. At the time, I thought nothing of it. She was simply a young, "cool" teacher. Nothing inappropriate happened. However, looking back at the situation, I now realize that she took a risk, albeit at that time a small one. Today, that would be a huge risk.

Social Networking

Educators' involvement in social networking also poses new challenges for school districts. There have been many cases throughout the country where educators have been threatened for dismissal because of Facebook content. King explains that the basic premise is that educators' free speech cannot be curbed unless their conduct compromises their ability to be role models.

However, young educators who grew up with social media may not comprehend or consider the ramifications of publishing certain content online in social forums like Facebook or a personal blog. People will write things, blog things, or text things that they would never say face-to-face. Goldstein's advice is concise and easy to understand: If you would be uncomfortable having your words printed on the front page of The New York Times, then don't write them down!

Imagine the scenario where a parent takes issue with an educator and deliberately searches the Internet, including Facebook, to try to validate their negative perception. The image that the educator puts forth on social networking sites defines that educator's identity.

Goldstein alleges that there is a perception of anonymity online that encourages a level of intimacy. Privacy settings create a sense of security. The reality is that most of our online interactions are held by third party providers. What we learned in the wake of 9/11 was that many of these providers caved and gave over information when pushed. Anonymity does not shield people. The idea that what we post online cannot be traced back is not true.

Students, Cell Phones, and Cameras

There is a camera in the student's pocket. Most of us have seen or heard of educators being caught on a student's cell phone video camera behaving in a compromising way and then having that video show up online in places like YouTube.

In large classrooms, it's almost impossible to catch every student using their phone during instruction. Educators must presume that they are under a technological microscope all the time.

In my work as an educator's coach, I have observed students using their phones in the classroom while the teacher was not looking. They put their purse or backpack on the desk and text message with their hands inside the bag. Students can easily record the teacher's voice in this manner. In addition, if a teacher is in a verbal confrontation with another student, that educator is likely not paying attention to the camera that might be pointing at him from across the room.

Attorney Pamela Parker of Austin, Texas, agrees. She warns that being recorded is the number one danger for educators right now. Even students who do not have malicious intent are recording things that they think are funny. They forward the video or post to everyone or online. This is much more dangerous because what has been recorded can be out of context, yet some people think that what is recorded is the truth. Kids treat it as a parlor trick - "OK, I have this statement, what can I turn it into?"

Allow Time for Reflection

Educators should be acting and speaking in a professional way - always. The informality that our society is moving towards cannot invade an educator's professional demeanor.

Take the Time to Think Before Responding

No matter how urgent you or anyone else believes an issue is, take the time to think before you respond. When asked to speak about someone, take the time to marshal your speculations and consider your words carefully. Parker shares an example from her experience: An upset parent comes to talk to you about an incident without an appointment. Educators need to know that it is OK to say, "I understand your concern. I want to help you. Let me consider this and I will get back to you." In addition, sometimes, the educator should not be the one addressing the issue. Educators need to know that they can be attentive to a parent without getting into a conversation in that moment. Educators need to speak with an "office type" demeanor.

In Conclusion

Since the days of Socrates, educators have been taught to consider the profound effect of their words. Despite the revolutionary changes in teaching strategies and the explosion of communicative technologies and social networks, those lessons still apply today. You may think that these caveats may affect the quality of your teaching. Perhaps you see them straitjacketing your behavior in and out of the classroom. On the contrary, use them as guidelines to sharpen your professional performance and to ensure that your words and actions reflect the gifts that you bring to the classroom.

Contributors:

Diana D. Halpenny, Attorney at Law, Kronick, Moskovitz, Tiedemann & Girard, Inc.
Pamela Parker, Attorney at Law, Austin, Texas
Bradford A. King, Attorney at Law, Thompson McMullan, P.C.
Mark Joel Goldstein, Attorney at Law, Milwaukee, WI

Data Collection Form 1 – Elementary

Student Initials:	Date:	Grade:
Classroom teacher:		
How was the student's day?	☺ ☺ ☹ Other?	

Time	Grouping (circle)	Student Behavior (How did he/she do?)	Activity	✓
	I S W		Phonics/Phonemic Awareness	
	I S W		Word Identification	
	I S W		Comprehension	
	I S W		Vocabulary (meaning emphasis)	
	I S W		Spelling/Mechanics	
	I S W		Oral Language	
	I S W		Reading: Choral, Guided, Partner, Independent	
	I S W		Math: Computation, Organization	
	I S W			
	I S W			

I – Individual   S – Small Group   W – Whole Class

When was the student engaged or not engaged in the class activities? What worked?	
What supplemental materials worked?	
How did the student engage with peers?	
How did the student respond to testing situations?	
How did the student do during unstructured time? (Recess, Hall, Cafeteria, etc.)	

Data Collection Form 2 – Secondary

Student Initials:	Date:		Grade:
Classroom teacher:			

| How was the student's day? | ☺   ☺   ☹ Other? | | |

Time	Grouping (circle)	Student Behavior (How did he/she do?)	Activity	✓
	I S W		Phonics/Phonemic Awareness	
	I S W		Word Identification	
	I S W		Comprehension	
	I S W		Vocabulary (meaning emphasis)	
	I S W		Spelling/Mechanics	
	I S W		Oral Language	
	I S W		Reading: Choral, Guided, Partner, Independent	
	I S W		Math: Computation, Organization	
	I S W			
	I S W			

I – Individual   S – Small Group   W – Whole Class

When was the student engaged or not engaged in the class activities? What worked?	
What adaptations worked?	
How did the student respond to testing situations?	
How did the student do during unstructured time?	
General Behavioral Comments	

Suggestions for the Daily Schedule

Once you have defined your roles in the classroom, the next step is to determine a manageable schedule. This schedule will vary from paraprofessional to paraprofessional depending upon:

- The grade level in which the paraprofessional is working.
- Whether the paraprofessional is a one-on-one student assistant.
- Whether the paraprofessional is working with an entire class to support students on an IEP.
- Whether the paraprofessional is in a secondary education situation, working with various teachers in various subjects over the course of a school day and supporting any number of students with special needs.

The paraprofessional and the general education teacher need time to sit down and communicate what this schedule shall look like.

Scheduling in the Elementary School

At the elementary level, it is important to prepare a schedule collaboratively that addresses:

- The teacher's classroom goals and schedule for the day.
- The assignments, activities, and tasks that the teacher intends to instruct over the course of the day.
- Areas in which the student or students may need assistance.
- Areas in which the teacher may need support in meeting student needs.

Scheduling at the Secondary Level

At the secondary level, the paraprofessional often moves between several classes during the course of a school day. In the role of a one-on-one student assistant, the paraprofessional will follow the student through most periods of the school day, except for the paraprofessional's own lunchtime. In a one-on-one position, the student's specific needs might be the most critical factor in determining how time is scheduled in each one of those classes.

When paraprofessionals are moving between classes it is more challenging to make time for collaboration between the general education teacher and the paraprofessional to sort out this schedule. The benefits, however, of investing time in designing a meaningful schedule, whether it be before class starts, at the beginning of the week, or at the beginning of a unit of instruction, are that the paraprofessional will be able to:

- Assist the teacher more effectively
- Schedule times for the student to be independent in his or her work situation
- Ensure that there are social interactions so that the student grows emotionally and socially
- Coordinate activities so that things run smoothly

Other times, the paraprofessional may be working with a variety of students over the course of the school day, serving the needs of several students on an IEP in the class. The paraprofessional is often working with many different personalities, over the course of each day. Each teacher will have his or her own scheduling concerns, priorities, and needs. It is important that these scheduling issues within the class period are discussed and worked out so that everyone wins.

How do you go about managing both the time for communication and the schedule? Use the checklists and forms included in this section as guides to decide the different aspects of the paraprofessional's role in the classroom. This step is critical to scheduling time.

Once a schedule is set, there are still times when a paraprofessional may feel that his or her time is not well spent. If the paraprofessional feels that time is being wasted, or that his or her professional skills are not being used, he or she may use this time to perform other activities that can support classroom goals. Refer to paraprofessional roles or jobs for suggestions on how to maximize class time, or consider the following options:

- Start to accumulate a binder of the course content for the students to match up their work against.
- Observe a student or collect behavioral data.
- Write down comments or discussion items to review collaboratively with the classroom teacher or special educator.
- Move about the room and use position control to make sure students in the class are on task, understanding their work, or behaving appropriately.
- Consider the concepts being taught in the classroom at that time and think of reinforcement activities for memorization and recall, review and practice, or re-teaching that could benefit students on an IEP and possibly, all students in the class.

Sample Secondary Level Daily Schedule – Multiple Locations

Time	Location	Subject	Support Function	Supervising Teacher
8:30-8:40	Front Foyer	N/A	Pick up student from bus	N/A
8:45-9:30	Hall B Room 23	Language Arts	Inclusion Classroom – Re-teach, read aloud with students	J. Smith
9:25-10:35	Hall C Room 14	Social Studies	One-on-one assist for M. T.	H. Gingras
10:40-11:25	Hall B Room 24	Language Arts	Inclusion Classroom – Re-teach, read aloud with students	J. Smith
11:30-12:15	Lunch			
12:20-1:05	Hall C Room 18	Social Studies	Inclusion Classroom – Provide small group and individual support as needed.	E. Sanchez
1:10-1:55	Resource Room	N/A	Provide tutorial support. Re-teach study skills. Drill and reinforcement.	R. Littledove
2:00-2:50	Hall B Room 23	Language Arts	Inclusion Classroom – Re-teach, read aloud with students	J. Smith

Secondary Level Daily Schedule – Multiple Locations

Time	Location	Subject	Support Function	Supervising Teacher

Sample Elementary Level Daily Schedule – Single Location

Time	Subject	Support Function	Notes
8:30-8:40	N/A	Pick up student from bus	
8:45-10:00	Reading	Re-teach, read aloud with students	
10:00-10:15	Recess	Supervise on the playground	
10:15-11:25	Language Arts	Re-teach, lead small group	
11:30-12:00	Lunch		
12:00-12:40	Specials	Inclusion Classroom – Provide small group and individual supports as needed.	
12:40-1:00	Science	Provide tutorial support. Re-teach study skills. Drill and reinforcement.	
2:00-2:50	Social Studies	Re-teach, read aloud with students, play review game	
2:50-3:15	Dismissal Routines	Engage students in activities while waiting to be called for dismissal	

Elementary Level Daily Schedule – Single Location

Time	Subject	Support Function	Notes

How Do I Follow-Up Outside of Class?

Sample Letters to Assist with Follow-Up at the Secondary Level

The following letters are helpful for paraprofessionals working within an academic support class environment. Frequently, students come to the class without their work. Gathering information about missing assignments helps the paraprofessional work more effectively with students.

Date:

Dear (Teacher's name),

(Student's name) is in (Study Hall, Resource Room, Support Lab, etc.) _____ class period. Would you please let me know if there is work missing or due for your class? It will assist me greatly in helping him/her to be successful in your class. If you feel that this student could benefit from any ongoing re-teaching, that information would be helpful as well. I appreciate your assistance.

Sincerely,

(Paraprofessional's name)

Paraprofessionals and Teachers Working Together

A special educator may struggle to keep up with how students are performing in general education classes, especially if those classes are not co-taught. A letter like this one might be sent to teachers periodically to get feedback on individual students. Be careful not to inundate the general education teacher with too many of these all at once, or too often.

Date:

Dear (Teacher's name),

(Student's name) is in your _____ period class, and has (Study Hall, Resource Room, Support Lab, etc.) _____ class period. If you could take a moment to fill out the information below it will assist me greatly in helping this student succeed in your class.

Please Circle One:
1. Estimate Grade: A   B   C   D   F
2. Turns in Homework: Always   Sometimes   Never
3. Tests/Quizzes: High   Average   Low   Failing
4. Do you feel this student could benefit from any ongoing re-teaching activities?   Yes   No

If Yes, please explain.

5. Is this student missing any assignments/tests that need to be made up/completed?   Yes   No

If Yes, please provide details.

Thank you for taking the time to complete this form!

Sincerely,

(Paraprofessional's name)

"Quick Form" Letter to Teachers to Assist with Follow-Up

This form allows a general education teacher to provide feedback on one form rather than many. List student names alphabetically so that teachers can align the list with the grade book.

Date:

Dear (Teacher's name),

The following students are in your _____ period class and have (Resource Room, Study Skills, Study Support, etc.). If you could take a moment to fill out the form below, it would assist me greatly in helping these students succeed in your class.

Please return to (Paraprofessional's name) by (date).

Student Name	Est. Grade	Missing Homework?	Missing Tests/Quizzes?	Assignments/Tests that need to be made up or completed	Comments

Thank you for taking the time to complete this form!

Sincerely,

(Paraprofessional's name)

Keeping Up With the IEP

Class List Adaptations Chart

I was a high school special education teacher when I started co-teaching. Consequently, I was often co-teaching with two to three teachers in the course of the day. Class sizes ranged from 25 to 32 students per class period. In each classroom, we might have up to thirteen students on an IEP. We would review the IEP in August before students arrived; however, trying to remember 45 to 65 student IEP's was impossible.

To ensure that we were meeting the needs of our students, I developed this class list adaptations chart as a cheat sheet so that we could quickly look at a class of students and know exactly what they needed daily. It worked beautifully.

Here are some important points regarding this chart.

1. At the top of the chart, in the row across each column, put a code for each student in the class who is on an IEP, 504 plan, RTI plan, etc. You might also put the student's initials if you feel that the initials would not identify specific students to anyone but you. The key is to use a naming system that does not identify the student. If this chart was found by someone who did not have the right to know that students' information, it would be a confidentiality violation.
2. After reading the IEP, check the items that apply to each specific student. The downloadable forms available to you through the download link provided at the beginning and at the end of this book are customizable. By using the downloadable forms, you can create checklists that are specific to your students.
3. A data collection option is to put a date in the checkbox so that there is a record of any adaptations or accommodations that have been made for specific students and which day they were provided.

Now, when giving a test, the teacher or specialist can look at this list and quickly identify students who need extra time, an oral test, or a modified test.

Following is an example of the type of form that will be available to you in the download collection offered to you as a supplement to this book.

Adaptations and Learning Profile - One Page View

						⟳ Student Initials/⟲Information
						Tests: Retake
						Tests: Extra Time
						Tests: Oral
						Tests: Modified
						Tests: Scribe
						Write Assignments on Board
						Monitor Assignment Notebook
						Break Down Assignments into Steps
						Provide Copies of Notes
						Substitute Hands-On for Written
						Substitute Oral for Written
						Seating Preference
						Allow Word Processor
						Allow Calculator
						Allow Text-to-Speech Software
						Allow Speech-to-Text Software
						Provide Advanced Organizer
						Needs One-on-One Assistance
						Visual Cues & Hands-on Critical
						Easily Overwhelmed
						Distractible
						Written Expression Weak
						Verbal Expression Weak
						Auditory Learner
						Visual Learner
						Kinesthetic Learner

Chapter 1 Review & Discussion Questions

Reflect and Write: For the Teacher

Take a moment to consider how you work with paraprofessionals and list approaches and areas that you would like to improve or learn more about by the end of this course.

Currently I....	I want to improve...

Reflect and Discuss: Paraprofessional Roles

- After reading this chapter, in what ways might paraprofessionals be underutilized in your classroom?
- List the ways that paraprofessionals are well utilized in your classrooms? What are they?
- What are some of the challenges you anticipate with altering your method of incorporating the paraprofessional into the environment?
- Brainstorm other ways you feel that paraprofessionals could assist in the classroom. Pair with a partner to share some of these actionable items. Add them to your checklists from the chapter on the blank lines as appropriate.

Reflect and Discuss: Tips for Success

- How have your attitudes changed towards the responsibilities of the paraprofessional after reading this chapter?
- What are some of the legal considerations for your state, county, district, and/or campus that you need to be familiar with to avoid putting the paraprofessional into compromising situations?
- Select up to three items from the "Tips for Success" pages that you feel you already do well.
- Select three items from the "Tips for Success" pages that you feel could use improvement.

Activity: Para/Teacher Communication Starter Form

Create a script that addresses at least two concerns from each sub-section of the form offered in the chapter. Format the script to model a sample conversation.

Once this is finished, trade scripts with another participant and role-play the conversational script. Then discuss potential areas of difficulty.

Reflect and Discuss: The Daily Schedule, Following Up Outside of Class, and Keeping Up with the IEP

- Describe how you could adapt or use some the forms from the chapter to increase communication between teachers, paraprofessionals, parents, administrators, coaches, or others involved in the student's education.

Take it to the Classroom - Practical Application:
Remember the three items in the "Tips for Success" pages that you previously considered for improvement? Now is your chance to create a plan of action to improve them!

Open a dialogue with your paraprofessional or teacher partner using some of the questions from the **Para/Teacher Communication Starter Form.**

If possible, implement the agreements made in the process of filling out the form for a week, then meet again to reflect on what worked and what didn't work.

Based on this information, create a new plan of action that addresses any concerns. Then plan a time to discuss concerns for the future.

✷ CHAPTER 2 ✷

How to Collaborate Successfully

Collaboration Approaches

Collaborative Roles in the Classroom

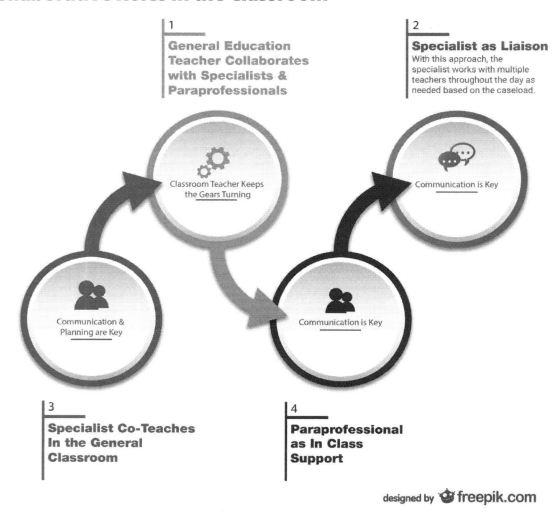

1

General Education Teacher Collaborates with Specialists & Paraprofessionals

Classroom Teacher Keeps the Gears Turning

2

Specialist as Liaison
With this approach, the specialist works with multiple teachers throughout the day as needed based on the caseload.

Communication is Key

3

Specialist Co-Teaches In the General Classroom

Communication & Planning are Key

4

Paraprofessional as In Class Support

Communication is Key

designed by 🎨 freepik.com

General Education

Given the magnitude of demands placed on classroom teachers today, they can become overwhelmed with the task of trying to meet the needs of a heterogeneously grouped co-taught classroom. Whereas some content area teachers are skilled in working with students with disabilities, and some may even have certification in special education, we cannot assume a general education teacher has that knowledge and background. Even when a teacher "can" meet the demands of today's' rigorous standards as well as the needs of their students, the opportunity to collaborate with specialists to meet student needs significantly increases the level of student success.

Specialist as Liaison

At times, the specialist acts as 'consultant' to the general classroom teacher. The special education 'consultant' works primarily outside the classroom with the general education teacher and may work directly in classrooms as needed. The general classroom teacher in this situation makes most, if not all, of the classroom adaptations, accommodations, and modifications, using the IEP and the special educator as a guide and resource.

Specialist Co-teaches in the General Classroom

Special education teachers can play a critical role in helping classroom and content area teachers analyze the standards-based lesson plan and design lessons that support all learners in the classroom. State Standards place new demands on content area teachers as well as special education teachers. It's important that both teachers take an active role in professional development that enables the special education teacher to become skilled in the content, as well as enabling the general education teacher to understand how to differentiate lesson plans and deliver Specially Designed Instruction (SDI) when necessary.

Paraprofessional as in-Class Support

If a paraprofessional is assigned to the general classroom, the special education teacher or specialist works closely with both the paraprofessional and the general classroom teacher.

Potential Roadblocks: Challenges

What are some of the problems, or obstacles, that come up between the paraprofessional and the classroom teacher that make it difficult to work together?

Teaching (and Re-teaching) Methodology

One roadblock often evolves from a difference in how both approach teaching. One might think this would not be an issue for the paraprofessional as it sometimes is for the co-teacher; however, it is a problem when personalities clash in the way a classroom is run, or if the way a paraprofessional re-teaches or manages students within the classroom does not sit well with the teacher's personality style.

Personality Differences

For example, Bob, who was working with several different teachers through the course of the day, was exasperated because, in his opinion, one of the classrooms he was working with was totally out of control. The teacher had a more loosely structured style of managing the classroom than was Bob's preference. Bob preferred a structured and ordered room where kids worked quietly, were orderly, did not speak out, and essentially were what we would expect from a traditional classroom: well-behaved.

The loose structure of the classroom, however, made it less likely that students would be quiet or stay in their seats for any length of time. This drove Bob crazy. It created stress and conflict because he felt powerless in his position to do anything about it.

Following is another example of a situation that is potentially a conflict. A classroom teacher with very unequivocal ideas about how teaching should happen in the classroom and what help a student should or should not get is paired with a paraprofessional who will do anything and everything he or she can do to get students to do the work. That might include cajoling, bribing, doing half of the work for them, talking to students (while the teacher is presenting) to try to convince them to get work done, etc.

There are potential problems in either scenario, but when the two adults in the room are so very different in their approach to teaching, or re-teaching, it is difficult to find a balance. Communication is the best solution. The paraprofessional, however, does not often feel confident in his or her ability to have that conversation because he or she often concludes, "It is not my class, so I cannot say anything about it."

Comfort Zones

Comfort zones are another significant factor in whether a relationship will be compatible. Many times, we are asked to do things in the classroom that are outside the comfort zone of either the teacher or the paraprofessional in the classroom. Possibly, the IEP requires the paraprofessional or the classroom teacher to use strategies that are unusual or unfamiliar. Or perhaps one of the two adults may not be comfortable having another adult in the room. On the other hand, given professional differences, one may not be comfortable being the other person in the classroom. When we are out of our comfort zones, we struggle.

Legal Worries

Sometimes, the general education teacher is concerned about not meeting the educational needs of students with disabilities or the IEP requirements adequately. This is especially true when students have significant disabilities or physical disabilities. This can create a roadblock because the paraprofessional may become the sole provider of all teaching and assistance for that student, or may even be the sole source of communication for that student.

Sometimes the teacher will feel more comfortable saying, "You take care of Johnny, because you know how to deal with Johnny and I don't. I'm not a special education teacher." This is caused by a concern that he cannot meet the student's needs or that legally he could get into trouble if he takes responsibility and then cannot meet that responsibility according to the standards of the law. This belief often feeds into the attitude of "Those sped kids are yours."

Even if the paraprofessional is a one-to-one assistant in the classroom, the general education teacher is ultimately responsible for the education of the child.

This Is Not the Way It Should Be

Another area of conflict and another roadblock to overcome when two adults work in a classroom together is differences in teaching styles. Sometimes, both enter the room with specific ideas of how the class should operate and how things should be. However, there is often a misperception about what is happening in the classroom, especially in the case where there has been little to no communication between these two adults prior to the first day of classes. Moreover, if class is not proceeding the way one or both thinks that it should, there is a problem. Again, communication is paramount in this situation. Communication simply must happen.

Feelings of Intimidation

At times, a general classroom teacher may be intimidated by a paraprofessional with a strong personality in the classroom. However, more often, the paraprofessional is the one who feels intimidated in that situation because of the potentially powerless position he or she holds. Communication can help to alleviate concerns that may arise regarding feelings of intimidation.

In my role as a consultant, I have often heard paraprofessionals share stories of their unhappiness in the classroom and their unwillingness to communicate with the classroom teacher about their concerns. The classroom teacher can help with this situation immensely by periodically asking the paraprofessional how he or she is doing. Asking paraprofessionals if they are they getting what they need, or how things could work better in the classroom for both the paraprofessional and the student with special needs, simply creates opportunities for more comfortable communication.

By being proactive, the general education teacher can minimize the amount of conflict in the classroom and increase the efficacy of the working relationship by simply checking in with their paraprofessional(s) on a regular basis. This does not need to be an hour-long meeting. This can be done in two minutes here, three minutes there, or while passing in the hall and chatting for a few minutes; whatever it takes. It is worth the investment in time. It is worth asking.

Credibility

Another roadblock that frequently comes up when general education teachers are working with paraprofessionals is one of credibility. Frequently, a paraprofessional is thrown into the classroom without any training. Unfortunately, the classroom teacher may not even be aware of the paraprofessional's strengths or areas of expertise, his or her background, or ability to meet the requirements of the job.

The classroom teacher needs and wants a paraprofessional who can simply come in and do the job well. Unfortunately, this does not always happen. The key to this dilemma is training. The classroom teacher or the special educator needs to take the time to share expectations with the paraprofessional, to explain the teaching methods being used, and to teach the paraprofessional how to use those methods.

Insufficient Time

If I have heard it once, I have heard it 100 times: there is simply not enough time to prepare materials for students, to meet with the teacher to learn strategies, or to get anything done proactively for the classroom. So often, paraprofessionals are sent from room to room with barely enough time to eat lunch or take care of their personal needs.

If we want paraprofessionals to be effective with students with special needs in the classroom, we need to change our paradigms about planning and prep time. Districts need to take into consideration the time that paraprofessionals need to have to gain the skills we expect them to acquire for working with our students' special needs.

Some districts address this issue by holding monthly trainings for paraprofessionals within the school day. Paraprofessionals are released from their responsibilities for one or two hours of the school day to attend training. The training can be led by a master teacher or experienced paraprofessional so that bringing someone in from the outside is not always necessary. This practice enables new and less experienced paraprofessionals to gain knowledge during the workday.

In the situation of a one-to-one assistant, release time may be more difficult to accomplish. Creative solutions may need to be considered. It is possible that a substitute who has the same period free will be able to cover for that paraprofessional. Alternatively, maybe another adult in the building would be willing to cover.

There are solutions to almost every issue, and those solutions are worth looking into, especially when finding the solution means that the paraprofessional will have the skills to be more successful in the classroom, with students overall, and in their relationships with the classroom teacher.

Lack of Administrative Support

Administrative support can also be a roadblock to the success of the paraprofessional working in the general education classroom. Sometimes this is simply because administrators have been unable or unwilling to provide paraprofessionals with training, time to communicate with their teachers, or even time to prep re-teaching materials. Funding can be an obstacle if there are limited monies available to provide quality training and follow-up. At times, there is a lack of support for inclusion efforts and for implementing the differentiated instruction necessary to meet the goals of current legislation. Other times, an administrator may simply have no voice among teachers to say loud and clear, "This is a legal requirement. We need to do it and you are accountable."

Potential Roadblocks: Other Practicalities

- At times, there is insufficient time & flexibility.
- It can be difficult to see lesson plans ahead of class time.
- There is often a lack of training in a problem-solving approach to collaboration.
- Cost of training and staffing minimizes available opportunities for professional development.
- What might you add?

Overcoming Roadblocks: Solutions

Being Flexible

Foremost, flexibility is a necessary trait for the paraprofessional. It is also an important quality for the general education teacher in an inclusive classroom. This can be a difficult requirement because our personalities are not always innately flexible. Some of us find it easier to go with the flow and take things as they come or to let things roll off our backs than others do. In the working relationship between a paraprofessional and teacher, without flexibility, there is rigidity. With rigidity, there is often a strained relationship. Be flexible and life will be easier and your students will be better served.

Identify and Focus on One's Strengths

The teacher has strengths in the classroom. The paraprofessional also has strengths. Find those strengths and celebrate them. This may be one of the most viable solutions to lack of training. If we find our strong points, we can work with those assets without requiring additional training. It is a logical solution to a common difficulty.

Adopt a "They are all our students" Attitude

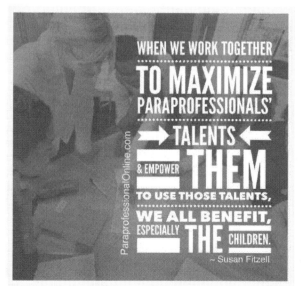

This is not only critical for the paraprofessional, but also extremely important for the students with special needs within the classroom. It is especially important to work with students in the general classroom in such a way that students with special needs are not stigmatized. Stigmatization as a "sped kid" leaves scars that can last a lifetime.

When the paraprofessional takes on the ownership of a student and the general classroom teacher leaves all interactions for that student to the paraprofessional, everyone loses. The teacher does not develop a potentially rewarding relationship with the student. The student becomes overly dependent upon the paraprofessional, having less social interaction with other students and less interaction with another adult. The student with special needs knows he or she is being ignored or left out by the general education teacher, which reinforces feelings of inferiority.

Overcoming Roadblocks: Summary & More

- Be flexible
- Identify and focus on teacher/paraprofessional strengths
- Adopt a "They are all OUR students" attitude
- Be self-aware
- Assess your viewpoints of the teaching profession
- Reflect on past experiences with change
- Understand your stage of life and career goals
- Consider gender and culture's impact on the relationship between you and the other adult in the classroom
- What is the perception of the particular change being considered?
- Increase your understanding of personality types

Perceptions & Personality

Looking at Personality Types

One of the most difficult aspects of working in the classroom with another adult is navigating personalities. Any time we work in a classroom, whether because of the personality of the students or the personality of the adults, we will face challenges due to our differences. It is important to understand your students' personalities and how their personalities influence how they learn. When we understand how students learn, we can be more helpful to our students by teaching them to identify how they learn and enabling them to learn to their maximum capability using strategies that fit their instructional needs.

Most of us realize the importance of understanding how students learn, and possibly even understand the importance of having an awareness of different personalities. However, this aspect of relationships is often glossed over or completely ignored in school environments.

In industry, managers, human resource departments, trainers, and team builders commonly understand the importance of understanding personality types. Sometimes businesses will even group people based on the best fit between different personalities. Schools tend to pair people together and expect them to figure out how to collaborate and work together with virtually no training or insight into personality theory, group process, or negotiation.

When I started working with other teachers in the classroom, I quickly discovered that one of the most critical lessons I needed to learn was to understand personality styles. What was most critical was understanding my own personality and how my personality affected others.

When I spoke with my 'demonstrative body language,' with every bit of 'passion' that I shared, with my 'extraversion' emphasizing every aspect of who I was, I intimidated people or overwhelmed some without even knowing it. It became clear to me that without an understanding of personality, I would continue to have relationships in the classroom that were not as productive as they could be. Too much time was spent misinterpreting each other, misunderstanding motivation, and sometimes taking those misunderstandings much too personally.

Working with a paraprofessional in the classroom requires the same amount of understanding and insight about personality. Everyone is different; some people approach the world from a logical standpoint, whereas some people approach the world from a values and harmony standpoint. Some people think and then speak. Some people speak and then think. Some need closure and make quick decisions; others want to keep their possibilities open. It helps when we understand personalities.

Let us look at some personalities that we might work with in the classroom. Here are some vignettes from my own experience.

(Names of the following personalities are changed to protect confidentiality.)

Meet Elaina

Elaina is a strong woman who exudes confidence and knows exactly what she believes in. Elaina works with students in the classroom as if it is her personal mission in life. She keeps up with each student and knows everything he or she is required to do. She does this completely without being told how or when to follow-up. Elaina's organizational skills put everyone else to shame. She keeps a binder for every classroom in which she works. These big, blue binders have dividers for every bit of notes, every test, and every piece of information students are required to have. She keeps notes on the students regarding their IEP goals and requirements. She also keeps a sample binder against which her students can check their work. She leaves these binders – minus the confidential information – in a public place so that people can access them and benefit from them. Elaina does not hesitate to tell anyone she works with exactly how she feels about a situation. If she is offended, you will know it. If she likes you, you will know it. In addition, she will not take any excuses from anyone, especially the students. Elaina is caring, strong, and passionate.

Meet Kay

Kay is quiet and a bit timid. Kay comes into the classroom silently, sits down, and scopes out the room. When she sees that a student might need help, Kay will discretely move over to that student's side of the room and, in a voice that is barely discernible, she will begin to tutor that student. She carries herself with elegance and exudes the utmost respect and dignity in everything she does. Kay knows her material and gets work done, but she will not deal with complex issues. If there are behavioral issues in the classroom, Kay will wait for the classroom teacher to manage it or she will ignore it. Kay cares deeply about her students; however, she is uncomfortable in the role of a disciplinarian.

Meet Maggie

Maggie has been working many years as a paraprofessional. Maggie's own children had learning challenges, so she has navigated the system from the viewpoint of a parent, not just from the perspective of a paraprofessional. She understands her students and the teachers she is working with. She manages to find a way to tell people exactly what she thinks and communicates what she needs in a manner that is never offensive, always loving, and is simply amenable. Maggie knows exactly when someone needs a perk and will share a little card, a thank you, a small gift, or a piece of chocolate with whomever she works. Maggie is a leader that takes initiative.

Meet Ellen

Ellen is new in her position. Ellen has not worked closely with children before apart from her own. She cares deeply, but feels a little uncomfortable in the teacher's classroom. She is unsure of what to do and when to do it because she is extremely concerned about offending the teacher or doing something wrong. Classroom disruption bothers her. Rude students offend her, yet her big heart pushes her to continue to strive, learning to help the students and the teachers in the classroom. Ellen needs to be told what to do every step of the way. When she understands her instructions, she does them willingly and the work is outstanding. Ellen needs some help learning teaching strategies. When watching Ellen give a test, sometimes it seems she gives just a little bit too much help. Ellen wants her students to succeed so badly that sometimes she does a little bit too much of the work for them.

Personality Preference and Learning

The MBTI®, Myers-Briggs Type Indicator® personality inventory, reports a person's preferred way of 'being' in the world and his or her preferred process for making decisions.

Characteristics of Personality Type (Myers-Briggs)

- There are polar opposites for each preference, and each is useful and important.
- Your preferences for certain mental habits are a persistent part of your personality.
- There are no good or bad types.
- Psychological type is not an intelligence test.
- Everyone is an individual; type only helps us understand part of our personality (and how we learn best).
- The MBTI is an indicator. It indicates preference. It is not a test.
- Following is a description of the four scales reported in the MBTI and several teaching approaches that will appeal to different MBTI profiles.

Extraversion (E) Versus Introversion (I)

This preference tells us how people "get their energy."

- Extraverts find energy in things and people. They prefer interaction with others, and are action-oriented. Extraverts are spontaneous thinkers who talk their thoughts aloud. Their motto is: Ready, Fire, Aim. For the extravert, there is no impression without expression.
- Introverts find energy in the inner world of ideas, concepts, and abstractions. They can be sociable, but need quiet to recharge their batteries. Introverts want to understand the world. Introverts concentrate and reflect. Their motto is: Ready, Aim, Aim... For the introvert, there is no impression without reflection.

"If you don't know what an extravert is thinking, you haven't been listening. But, if you don't know what an introvert is thinking, you haven't asked!"

Sensing (S) Versus Intuition (N)

This preference tells us how people take in information.

- Sensing types rely on their five senses. Sensing people are detail-oriented; they want facts and trust those facts.
- Intuition types rely on their imagination and what can be seen in "the mind's eye." Intuitive people seek out patterns and relationships among the facts they have gathered. They trust hunches and their intuition and look for the "big picture."

"Sensing types help intuitives keep their heads out of the clouds, while intuitives help sensing types keep their heads out of a rut."

Thinking (T) Versus Feeling (F)

This preference tells us how people make decisions.

- Thinking types prefer to decide things impersonally based on analysis, logic, and principle. Thinking students value fairness. What could be fairer than focusing on the situation's logic, and placing great weight on objective criteria in deciding?
- Feeling types prefer to make decisions by focusing on human values. Feeling students value harmony. They focus on human values and needs as they make decisions or arrive at judgments. They tend to be good at persuasion and easing differences among group members.

"Thinking types need to remember that feelings are also facts that they need to consider, while feeling types need to remember that thinking types have feelings too!"

Judging (J) Versus Perceptive (P)

This preference tells us people's attitudes towards the outside world.

- Judging types prefer to make quick decisions. Judging people are decisive, planful (they make plans), and self-regimented. They focus on completing the task, only want to know the essentials, and act quickly (perhaps too quickly). They plan their work and work their plan. Deadlines are sacred. Their motto is: Just do it!
- Perceptive types prefer to postpone action and seek more data. Perceptive people are curious, adaptable, and spontaneous. They start many tasks, want to know everything about each task, and often find it difficult to complete a task. Deadlines are meant to be stretched.
- Their motto is: On the other hand...

"Judging types can help perceiving types meet deadlines,
while perceiving types can help keep judging types open to new information."

MBTI Self-Assessment Table

Jung's Personality Preference Types

Extraversion _____ How you re-energize _____ **I**ntroversion
Energized by   Energized by
the outside world   the inner world

Sensing _____ How you take in information _____ i**N**tuition
Work with what   Looks for possibilities
is familiar and known   and relationships

Thinking _____ On what you base your decisions _____ **F**eeling
Decisions based on   Decisions are based
impersonal analysis & facts   on personal values

Judging _____ How you relate to the world externally _____ **P**erception
Prefer life to be   Prefer a flexible,
planned, decided, and orderly   spontaneous way of life

	E or I	S or N	T or F	J or P
Self Assessment Type				
Indicator Type				

After reading the previous pages, use this form to mark your preferences. What type do you think you are? What type does the Myers-Brigg's Indicator state as your preference? Is your preference in each function clear or slight?

If you have the opportunity to take the MBTI inventory, fill those preferences in the bottom row. Is there a difference between your self-assessment type and your MBTI inventory results? If there is, simply read descriptions of your Myers-Briggs preferences according to your self-assessed report and your Indicator reports. Which one fits your personality more? The MBTI inventory simply indicates your preferences. Only you can decide your personality type.

Remember, these results are not carved in stone. Use this information as a launching board to discover your type and gaining a deeper understanding of yourself and others.

The MBTI Type Table

ISTJ	ISFJ	INFJ	INTJ
ISTP	ISFP	INFP	INTP
ESTP	ESFP	ENFP	ENTP
ESTJ	ESFJ	ENFJ	ENTJ

The following chart, "Tip Sheet: How to communicate with..." may be used to determine how you might communicate with another personality type. For example, if you want to present a proposal to an INTJ, then you would be more successful in convincing the INTJ to accept the proposal if you:

- Give them time to process and reflect on what you are proposing.
- Develop alternative solutions rather than presenting just one option.
- Present information to INTJ with logic.
- Ensure closure. INTJ needs a decision; to leave without setting up a date to reach closure would be problematic for INTJ.
- Demonstrate your knowledge, competency, and credibility when presenting the proposal.

MBTI Tip Sheet: How to communicate with...

ISTJ	ISFJ	INFJ	INTJ
•Give them time to process & reflect •Know & present the facts •Present information with logic •Ensure closure – needs a decision •Present measured results & data	•Give them time to process & reflect •Know & present the facts •Understand people values •Ensure closure – needs a decision •Point out practical benefits	•Give them time to process & reflect •Develop alternative solutions •Understand people values •Ensure closure – needs a decision •Point out value to relationships	•Give them time to process & reflect •Develop alternative solutions •Present information with logic •Ensure closure – needs a decision •Demonstrate competency
ISTP	**ISFP**	**INFP**	**INTP**
•Give them time to process & reflect •Know & present the facts •Present information with logic •Be flexible •Present measured results & data	•Give them time to process & reflect •Know & present the facts •Understand people values •Be flexible •Point out practical benefits	•Give them time to process & reflect •Develop alternative solutions •Understand people values •Be flexible •Point out value to relationships	•Give them time to process & reflect •Develop alternative solutions •Present information with logic •Be flexible •Demonstrate competence
ESTP	**ESFP**	**ENFP**	**ENTP**
•Put agreements into words •Know & present the facts •Present information with logic •Be flexible •Present measured results & data	•Put agreements into words •Know & present the facts •Understand people values •Be flexible •Point out practical benefits	•Put agreements into words •Develop alternative solutions •Understand people values •Be flexible •Point out value to relationships	•Put agreements into words •Develop alternative solutions •Present information with logic •Be flexible •Demonstrate competence
ESTJ	**ESFJ**	**ENFJ**	**ENTJ**
•Put agreements into words •Know & present the facts •Present information with logic •Ensure closure – needs a decision •Present measured results & data	•Put agreements into words •Know & present the facts •Understand people values •Ensure closure – needs a decision •Point out practical benefits	•Put agreements into words •Develop alternative solutions •Understand people values •Ensure closure – needs a decision •Point out value to relationships	•Put agreements into words •Develop alternative solutions •Present information with logic •Ensure closure – needs a decision •Demonstrate competency

*The author of the chart "Tip Sheet: How to communicate with..."
is unknown.

When in Conflict

There are times in the classroom when there will be a conflict with the teacher with whom one is working. Alternatively, there will be times when a classroom teacher will have a problem or a conflict with a paraprofessional. How does a person handle that conflict in a constructive way? How does a person manage the relationship so that both can work together without offending or hurting each other? When situations get tough, one of the first things to remember is that when in conflict, it is most often about personality. That other person is not trying to "get" you.

What are we thinking when something happens in the classroom that triggers our frustration or our anger? Sometimes, we are thinking such things as, "That person should know better," or "I told her that she should do such and such, and she didn't listen to me!" or "Every time this happens in the classroom, she does that simply to annoy me." "She's an idiot." "He thinks he knows everything!" "He is a control freak. I can't stand him." Every one of these types of statements that we think to ourselves in times of conflict is negative self-talk. Negative self-talk begets more negativity, anger, frustration, and dissatisfaction.

What if we change our self-talk? What if, instead of saying, "This person is doing this to annoy me," we replaced that thought with, "She's trying her best. This is just her personality. How might I approach this personality that is so different from me in her approach to the world?" What if we simply say, "I can handle this," or, "This isn't about me, this is about him, and I need to know how to approach him."

When we can take a step back and look at this situation in terms of personality, it is much easier to handle conflicts in the classroom. Instead of taking things personally, we understand that it is simply about personality and a person's comfort level.

Once you have your positive self-talk – for example, you have told yourself, "I can handle this!" – start considering solutions to the problem. Seek the counsel of a respected colleague, or someone you know who really understands how to approach different personalities. You will find that person by looking for someone who seems to be able to work with just about anyone and who has an amazing understanding of people. Seek that person out and ask him or her how you might approach the problem. Ideally, you would do this without naming the person with whom you are having a problem.

There are many resources available to help people figure out what to say. In a difficult situation, use these resources. Albert Ellis has several books on the market that share strategies for handling difficult situations and feelings and suggesting ways to keep our minds in a rational and positive place. For example, just the title of his book, "How to Stubbornly Refuse to Make Yourself Miserable About Anything – Yes, Anything" (Paperback - July 1988) encourages a smile.

Consider using "I" statements to share how you feel about a situation. Avoid using the word "you" when communicating how you feel. Be careful to avoid blaming language. Even if you believe the other person is wrong, find a way to approach the conversation from a positive perspective. Once you figure out how you want to handle the problem, role-play a conversation with another trusted colleague or friend. Visualize the interaction in your mind. Practice what you will say until you feel confident. Visualize that you are successful in this interaction.

There are times when it is best to say nothing. That choice is more difficult for some personalities than for others. There are times it is important to speak up about our concerns, and that is easier for some personalities and more difficult for others. The most critical factor is that whatever we choose to do, we try to frame our actions, our words, and our thoughts in positive ways.

When in Conflict:
- Change negative self-talk to positive
- Consider "Next time X happens... I'll do Y or Z"
- Plan viable solutions
- Consider personality type
- Seek suggestions from a supportive colleague or read Albert Ellis for suggestions to reframe
- Visualize yourself in the interaction BEING SUCCESSSFUL!
- Affirm: "I CAN handle this situation"

Stop Conflict in Its Tracks!

Have you ever had people in your life who seem to enjoy baiting you? Have you wondered if all their amusement in life comes from trying to get a rise out of you? Have you ever found yourself in a conversation with a colleague, and, when the conversation finished, shaking your head, and asking yourself, "What was that all about?" Have you ever concluded, "I should have said this!" or "I should have said that!" Sometimes, we leave the conversations feeling defeated, and strangely so, because we are not always sure what happened.

Do you have someone you interact with who seems to have an answer for everything? What about someone who happens to be overly critical? How do we handle these types of conversations and these characters in our lives who challenge us with their words? Consider learning and using words and phrases that stop conflict in its tracks.

I remember a colleague of mine who was in the business world for his entire career. He loved to jibe me about being a teacher. Every time we got together, he would disparage the teaching profession. He knew I was a teacher and he loved to see my reaction. Of course, much to his pleasure, I reacted in passionate defense. Year after year, however, this became a tiresome tradition when we visited. Finally, one day, my colleague started in with his tirade about teaching and teachers in the profession, and I simply looked at him with a smile on my face and said, "You have an interesting perspective. I'll have to give that more thought." Then I changed the subject. Much to my amazement, his jaw dropped and he seemed to search for what to say next. It took the wind out of his sail and it was done so nicely.

Knowing phrases that stop conflict in its tracks is just one piece of the conflict-avoidance puzzle. The words we speak are less than 10% of our total communication. Body language and tone of voice are critical factors in how we communicate with other people. Body language communicates more than 80% of what we are trying to express. Tone of voice communicates more than 10% of what we are trying to convey.

So, if we have a comeback that should diffuse a conflict situation, such as "You have an interesting perspective. I'll have to give that some thought," the body language we use when we say those words and the tone of voice with which we speak them could render them either fighting words or words that diffuse a conflict situation. A calm and neutral tone of voice and relaxed body language will be the key factor as to whether the words stop conflict in its tracks.

Scripts for Stopping Conflict in Its Tracks

When you find yourself caught in a verbal exchange that does not 'feel' right, then you may be dealing with bullying — intimidation, bulldozing, sarcasm, etc.

You may, also, simply be dealing with someone who is upset over a misunderstanding and unable to communicate clearly in the moment.

Three Steps to Take Control of a Challenging Interaction:

- RECOGNIZE & PAY ATTENTION to your body signals — don't ignore the discomfort, adrenaline rush, etc.
- STOP, BREATHE, and THINK: "I CAN handle this!" (Positive self-talk)
- CONSCIOUSLY act! (As opposed to reacting.)

Keep Your Power

Be conscious of your body language and the words you choose:

Comebacks That Don't Escalate the Conflict

- I see.
- Thank you for letting me know how you feel.
- Perhaps you are right.
- I hear you.
- Ouch! (Cues the other person that they are being hurtful. Sometimes they don't realize.)
- I can see this upsets you.
- I'm sorry you were hurt. That was not my intent.
- I shouldn't have to defend myself, and I won't.
- Excuse me, I'm not finished. (Say softly).
- Agree with some of the statement but not all. (e.g. "You have a chip on your shoulder because you are short." Agree. Say, "Yes, I am short.")
- You have an interesting perspective.
- I'll have to give that some thought.
- I will talk to you when you are calm. (Call "Time" & leave).

71

- I will talk to you when I am calm. (Call "Time" & leave) Ask a question- S/he who asks the question has the power.
- Why does that bother you?
- How so?
- Why do you ask?
- What makes you say that?
- I know you wouldn't have said that unless you had a good reason. Could you tell me what it was?

Tips to Successfully Shift from Conflict to Calm Strength

- Be careful about tone of voice and/or lower your voice.
- Avoid "should," "ought," and "you" statements.
- Watch your body language. Respect personal space.
- Use "I statements" to communicate how you feel. Avoid accusatory language.

Tools for Collaborative Relationships

Communication: "What's Working?" Card

Good communication with co-workers and students is critical to successful inclusion. Sometimes, our fears, agendas, and even enthusiasm get in the way of doing the kind of listening we need to do to foster good communication. Without effective communication, we make many assumptions about the people with whom we interact. Those assumptions might be very inaccurate and create tremendous conflict. Try to keep an open mind. Express how you feel and listen to other viewpoints. Good communication is necessary for the success of an inclusive classroom.

It's Working!

Not Working as Well

Let's Try ...

This card is a simple way to give feedback to your co-workers or individual members of the teaching team. I found it to be useful for reinforcing the positives. It can be delivered in person, or placed in a teacher mailbox. Simple 3X5 index cards work well.

Phrasing Words for Positive Results

- What can I do to support you? How can I help make this challenge easier for you?
- Can we talk about something I think might help us work together better?
- I'd like to talk about...with you, but first I'd like to get your point of view.
- I think we may have different ideas about... I'd really like to hear your thinking on this and share my perspective as well.
- Be careful of your tone of voice...These two letters can mean something completely different depending on the tone of voice in which they are spoken. Oh! Oh? Ohhhhh.

More Tips for Successful Collaboration

- Be flexible
- Look for success, not only in academic areas
- Make time to plan — even if it's just 10 minutes!
- Discuss problems only with each other
- Avoid using red ink to write notes to your colleagues
- Pick-Me-Ups, Pick-U-Ups
- Compliment your colleagues where all can see
- Send a letter of appreciation and CC: the principal
- Remember special days with cards

Chapter 2 Review & Discussion Questions

Potential Roadblocks: Differences and Solutions

Reflect and Discuss

- What problems presented in this section do you resonate with?
- Choose one of the problems that you resonate with to focus on resolving with your collaborative partner. Create a plan, either independently or with your collaborative partner, to overcome those fears and concerns.

Perceptions & Personality

This section describes how personality affects the kinds of communication and collaboration that does, or sometimes doesn't, occur between people. It also provides a few personality case studies to use as examples of the personalities you will encounter in your career.

Reflect and Discuss

After reading the personality case studies, do you anticipate resonating or "butting-heads" with any of the personality types listed?

Personality Preference and Learning

This section introduces and explores the Myers-Briggs personality types, and different strategies for effectively communicating and collaborating with each type.

Reflect and Discuss

- Use the self-assessment table in this chapter to determine your personality type.
- How do you think your type impacts your relations with other paraprofessionals, other teachers, and administrators?
- How does your personality type impact your interaction with students with personality types that do not complement yours?
- Why is understanding different personalities important to establish effective collaboration?

When in Conflict & Stopping Conflict in Its Tracks

This section discusses effective strategies for stopping conflict and methods for turning the conversation into a productive, collaborative. discussion

Reflect and Discuss

Take a few minutes to think of any negative self-talk phrases that enter your thoughts during your interactions in the classroom. Work with a partner to replace these negative self-talk phrases with more neutral or positive self-talk phrases.

Consider one of the fears from the chapter that may contribute to communication conflict. Take a moment to visualize yourself being successful in the resolution of the conflict. Then, draw your visualization. (Stick figures and blob-people are entirely acceptable.)

OR

Create an acronym that will help you remember some of the comebacks that don't escalate the conflict.

❦ CHAPTER 3 ❧

Positive Behavior Management

Be a Positive Role Model

Role-modeling appropriate behavior is a vital and necessary component of an effective approach to behavior management.

Beliefs and Attitudes of the Role Model

Who we are, what we think, and what we believe is revealed through our words and behavior. If we buy into the adage "Boys will be boys," our words and behavior will reflect it. If we have prejudices, they will be apparent. Everything we say and do provides the foundation for children's belief systems and attitudes. Sometimes, we are not even conscious of what we believe. Many times, until we find ourselves reacting to a situation we feel strongly about, we do not really know that we have bought into a stereotype, a prejudice, or an attitude that limits us. Only when we become self-aware can we change our attitudes and beliefs to reflect the image we want our youth to model. Young people are more likely to do what we do, rather than what we say.

The Role Model and Discipline

Sometimes as teachers, parents, or adults in authority, we do not realize how we speak to children. Our tone of voice and choice of words, especially when disciplining, may be reinforcing negative patterns of behavior with children. This became glaringly obvious to me in my early years as a parent as I listened to my seven-year-old when she was angry with me. I often heard my words, my tone, and saw my facial expressions coming from her little body.

A small child does not categorize behavior. He does not say, "Oh, this is the tone I can use when I am an adult reprimanding my child." Rather, the behavior is interpreted as, "This is the tone I use when I am angry."

Traditionally, authoritarian discipline is used in schools and homes to manage children's behavior. An authoritarian approach, where directives and punishments are determined by the adult without enlisting the child in the formation of rules and consequences, produces youth who obey when in the presence of that adult. The downside to authoritarian discipline is that youth do not learn to self-discipline. They also learn to get what they want by using directives and meting out "punishments."

I do not advocate permissiveness; rather, I recommend an authoritative approach to discipline. An authoritative model involves students in the rule-making process. Consequences are established and firm limits on behavior are kept. An adult who uses an authoritative model of discipline is teaching students skills that are critical to sound character and conflict management.

When youth are involved in developing rules and consequences, they learn to use words to solve problems, to govern themselves, and to feel empowered. When rules deemed necessary by the adult are explained and consequences are logical, youth learn to be fair and trusting. When students who break the rules are involved in determining ways to "solve their own problem," they learn to control their own behavior. When young people are taught to see situations from another child's point of view and are required to make restitution to the hurt party, they learn empathy, forgiveness, and caring.

Discipline vs. Punishment: What's the Difference?[2]

PUNISHMENT	DISCIPLINE
▪ Punishment is <u>unexpected</u>. It is usually based on personal authority and arbitrary power.	▪ Discipline is <u>expected</u>. It is based on logical or natural consequences.
▪ Punishment is too severe.	▪ Discipline is fair and reasonable.
▪ Punishment reinforces failure. The individual has no options.	▪ Discipline reinforces success. Options are kept open as the individual is willing to take some responsibility.
▪ Punishment focuses on guilt, shame, blame, and fault.	▪ Discipline focuses on restitution and learning a better way.
▪ Punishment is meted out in the spirit of anger.	▪ Discipline is nurturing and caring.

---

[2] Based on work done by Diane Gossen, Perry Good, Barnes Boffey, and William Glasser.

Treat Youth with Respect

Lack of respect from our youth is a common complaint heard from adults today. I am often astounded, however, by the lack of respect some adults show towards young people. Youth are often treated as lesser beings. Children are ordered around without a "please" or a "thank you." Because they are defenseless, they are often the scapegoats of misplaced anger. Their needs are often disregarded. I have witnessed adults ridicule youth for their failures and poke fun at their shortcomings.

All of us may be guilty of disrespecting our children's rights sometimes when we are tired, frustrated, or angry. It must be the exception, not the rule. When we do treat young people in a disrespectful way, the most empowering thing we can do for our children, and for ourselves, is to admit we made a mistake. When we admit our errors to young people, we teach them that it is okay to make mistakes. Mistakes are for learning. We are modeling a willingness to be honest, to own our behavior, and to learn from it. This is a powerful example to set for our youth.

We Demonstrate Respect When We:

- Listen carefully when students speak. Remain open-minded and objective. Consider their messages carefully. Avoid interrupting a student or offering unsolicited advice or criticism.
- Respect students' personal space. Students may feel threatened and become agitated if you violate their personal space.
- Use friendly gestures, not aggressive ones. Avoid "finger-pointing." Open, upturned palms may be more appropriate and effective.
- Use preferred name. Ask each student how they would like to be addressed in the classroom. Only in rare instances would their chosen name be inappropriate.
- Get on their level. Try to adopt their physical level. If they are seated, try kneeling or bending over, rather than standing over them.
- Ask questions rather than make accusations. This assumes that the student is a responsible person. "Are you ready to begin?" rather than "Put your magazine away. It's time to start class." Use a concerned and kind tone.
- Address problem behaviors privately. Reprimanding students in front of their peers may embarrass them unnecessarily. Speaking to them privately helps preserve their integrity and self-esteem.

Paraprofessionals Have Limited Authority

Working Within the Paraprofessional's Jurisdiction

Paraprofessionals usually face an additional challenge in the classroom, cafeteria, and playground: they have limited authority. Paraprofessionals usually cannot impact student grades. They rarely can keep students after school or schedule time in the day to work out a behavior contract with a student. They are usually dependent on another adult or authority to carry out the discipline for the offense that happened in their care.

Unfortunately, these realities make it difficult for the paraprofessional to develop rapport as an authority figure with students. Consequently, the paraprofessional must choose disciplinary methods that are primarily collaborative and least likely to set the stage for a power struggle. This also allows the paraprofessional to develop a positive rapport with students.

Also, paraprofessionals should not be asked to contact parents about discipline problems that have occurred during the day. These should be discussed with the teacher or school administrator.

Violent Students: Proceed with Caution

Special training is required to properly diffuse situations involving students with a tendency towards violent outbursts. Physically violent students and students with serious emotional disturbance may need wrap-around services[7]. Paraprofessionals and teachers working with physically violent students need intensive specialized training to respond effectively to violent behaviors.

---

[7] A wrap-around support system is a collaborative effort involving agencies and schools to provide coordinated services to a student and/or a student's family.

General Behavior Management Tips

Behaviors to Avoid When Disciplining

- Shouting or continually nagging
- Pushing or pulling students about
- Confronting in an accusatory tone
- Engaging in banter/arguing
- Sarcasm
- Threatening (as opposed to presenting logical consequences or choices)
- Jumping to conclusions
- Assuming that students who are regularly in trouble are always to blame for incidents
- Losing your temper

Techniques That Build Rapport & Foster Better Behavior

- Treating students with respect
- Treating students in a firm, friendly, and quiet way
- Giving plenty of praise/rewards for appropriate behavior
- Making a note of all serious incidents that need follow-up
- Knowing where there is help in case of an emergency
- Dealing with matters consistently as set out in staff procedure or as agreed upon by responsible staff
- Keep a notebook to record good and poor behavior; this allows you to follow-up on all incidents
- Attempt to reprimand students quietly and privately

If you must discipline someone, make a determined effort to repair the relationship once the discipline is over.

Encourage Choice and Decision-Making

Offering students choices is the first line of defense for avoiding behavior problems. Additionally, five specific areas can be enhanced when individuals are allowed to make choices and decisions for themselves.

Benefits of Offering Choice:

- May reduce or prevent problem behaviors.
- Can offer independence.
- Can increase motivation and productivity.
- Can prevent learned helplessness.
- Can increase attention to task.

Scripts for Offering Choice

- You can do any ten questions/problems on page 103.
- Do the 'X' assignments in any order you choose.
- Choose 3 of 10 activities.
- Choose where to sit for independent activities.
- You may have a one-minute break now or a three-minute break in 10 minutes.
- When a student balks at an assignment, such as, "Write the spelling words three times each," you might respond, "Come up with a better plan to learn the material and present it to me."

Examples of Options to Offer for Choice-Making[8]

Type of Choice	Situation	Question Format
BETWEEN ACTIVITIES: Provide a choice between two or more activities during a routine	LIBRARY: Listen to a book on tape or ask the librarian to read a book out loud	CLOSED: Would you like to do your spelling or science? OPEN: Which subject would you like?
WITHIN ACTIVITIES/ MATERIALS: Provide a choice between two or more items within a specific task	SNACK: Apple or grapes SPELLING: Quiz a friend or write words out on a worksheet	CLOSED: Would you like an apple or grapes? OPEN: What type of fruit would you like?
REFUSAL: Before beginning a task, provide a choice of whether or not to participate	ACADEMICS: Do you want to complete the activity so that you have time to take part in the review game, or do you want to spend all of your time sitting out the activity alone?	CLOSED: Give two definite choices OPEN: Let student present options
WHO: At the beginning of a task, provide a choice of whom to work or play with	LUNCH: Would you like to sit with your friends or the teacher at lunch?	CLOSED: Same OPEN: With whom would you like to work?
WHERE: At the beginning of a task, provide a choice of where to do the activity	ACADEMICS: Would you like to sit at your desk or the study carrel to work?	CLOSED: Same OPEN: Where would you like to complete your reading assignment?
WHEN: Provide a choice of when to participate in an activity	ACADEMICS: Would you like to do your reading now or after gym?	CLOSED: Same OPEN: When would you like to go to the park?
TERMINATE ACTIVITY: Periodically during the task, provide the choice to quit	INDIVIDUAL WORK TIME: Let me know when you need to stop and take	CLOSED: Do you want to stop or continue? OPEN: Let me know when you

---

[8] Adapted from Bambara, L. M., & Koger, F. (1996). Self-scheduling as a choice-making strategy. In D. Browder (Ed.), Innovations: Opportunities for daily choice making (pp. 33-41). Washington, DC: American Association on Mental Retardation.

Scripts for Responding to Student Behavior

Sometimes, it helps to have an idea of how to respond to student behavior in a way that encourages students to own their actions, does not create a power struggle, and is consistent and effective.

> *Scripts should be stated in a calm tone of voice, with normal voice volume. Be careful not to get into the student's space; rather, convey non-threatening yet self-assured body language.*

Following are some suggestions for response. These scripts are just suggestions and are not guaranteed to work. Use your professional judgement when using the scripts because every student and situation is different.

For Disruption or Arguing

"Eric, that's disrupting. Yelling out 'A bunch of idiots are sitting on the porch!' could be offensive to some. Can you say that same thing in a way that may not be offensive?"

"Eric, that's arguing. What do you need to do if you think someone is 'getting into it with you'? Make a good choice for yourself."

"Eric, that's arguing. I need you to immediately stop in [five to ten seconds] or ... [state consequence]."

For Refusing to Work or Participate Appropriately

Say, "Eric, that's refusal. Might _____ be a better choice?"

If Eric responds positively, 'notice' the positive choice (reinforce).

If behavior continues...

Say, "Eric, that's continued refusal. What is it you were asked to do? Please make a good choice for yourself so the **adults** don't have to make it for you."

If Eric responds positively, 'notice' the positive choice (reinforce).

If behavior continues...

Say, "Eric, that's continued refusal. I need you to do what you were asked to do, or... [state the consequence]."

For Tardiness to Class

Say, "Eric, it is X minutes past the time you needed to be in class. That is tardiness. I need you to come to class on time. Can you do that?" (Give one or two chances, no more.)

Say, "Eric, it is X minutes past the time you needed to be in class. That is tardiness. You told me that you could be on time ... [yesterday, Monday, etc.] The consequence for tardiness is ... [state the consequence]. The next time you are tardy, you'll have a consequence."

For Having Difficulty Settling Down

- "You can _____ as soon as you get quiet. This offer is good for 10 seconds."
- "You can sit anywhere you like, as long as you don't block the door or interfere with anyone else's learning."
- "You can _____ as soon as you finish _____ section of your work."

For Bullying

- "I need you to use appropriate language. [state behavior] is hurtful. We don't hurt others in this class."
- "Those words [state what student said] embarrassed [name student]. Those words are hurtful.
- "We don't say [state what student said] in this class. Those words are hurtful. What's another way you can express how you feel? Would you like some options?" If yes, share possible options. If no, state possible consequences if behavior continues.

When the Student Attacks the Adult to Try to Turn the Tables

Student to adult: "You smell!"

Adult responds, in a matter-of-fact, firm tone of voice: "What's important in this conversation is your behavior (or what happened)." Then continue to address the student's behavior.

When Students Try to Debate (Don't Take the Bait!)

Adult: "Johnny, I need you to sit down."

Student: "Why do I have to sit down? Jane isn't sitting down!"

Adult: "Johnny, I need you to sit down."

Student: "Why? You are always picking on me!"

Adult: "Johnny, I need you to sit down."

Repeat in a calm, firm monotone until Johnny gets tired of hearing the 'broken record' and sits down.

A Note About Consequences

The challenge with consequences is that many times, paraprofessionals have limited authority or in-school time to follow through with consequences. Consequently, careful thought must go into what constitutes reasonable consequences for each situation.

I'm an advocate of authoritative discipline (as opposed to authoritarian) and restorative justice (as opposed to punishment). Ideally, consequences **teach and build relationship** between the student and the adult. Consequences that destroy relationships and don't teach or promote better choices are typically ineffective.

If detention is used as a consequence, spend the time to build rapport and teach, not preach, about good choices and how they might help him be more successful at getting what he wants.

Help Students Think Through Choices

Decision-Making Strategy: Problem-Solving Flowchart

I started using this problem-solving strategy(Fitzell, 2007) with students to help them see that there were positive and negative consequences to any solution they presented to a problem they were experiencing. Originally, it was used to help students who were dealing with anger towards another adult or student, and who were gravitating towards poor choices.

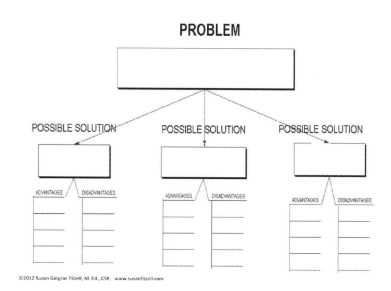

I discovered, over time, that this tool is a great way to help students with any decision-making process. Here's how it works...

Who: Student with a problem.

What: The use of the flowchart to brainstorm, analyze, and choose solutions to problems.

When:
- Student must make a decision and is having difficulty doing so.
- Teacher and student are experiencing a conflict or discipline issue. For example, a student must choose courses to take next semester, or must decide what after school activity to do; how to handle a difficult situation; or how to choose between any two options.

Why: All too often, students make decisions without thinking through the positive and negative consequences of those decisions. This flowchart allows students to work with an adult to come up with the best solution for the student.

Critical factor: Adults are encouraged to guide the student through this process without passing judgment, or trying to convince the youth that certain pros and cons are better than others, or certain decisions need to be made. It is imperative that the adult help the student brainstorm pros and cons, but not make the decision for the child or pressure the child to think of things in any one way.

Accommodation: Students may fill this chart out on their own, or an adult may scribe for the student.

For example, a student would come to me upset because another student bullied him. The first solution students would often choose was fighting. So, I would sit down with the student, list the problem on a piece of paper, create a T-chart, and start asking questions. If the first possible solution for that student was to beat up the antagonizer, I would simply write that down at the top of the first T-chart.

Next, I would ask the student to list the advantages of beating up the student they were angry with. Usually they came up with this list quite easily. I happily wrote these solutions down without passing judgment or discouraging their choices. I have learned through years of working with angry adolescents that the last thing they were willing to hear was my lecture on how they should behave and what better choices they might have available.

The next step was to write down the disadvantages of that solution. This is the part where students usually ran into trouble. Oftentimes, they could not think of any disadvantages, or they did not want to admit or list them.

If students could not come up with potential consequences to their solution, I would ask if they would like me to offer possible consequences. Typically, a student would allow me to suggest negative consequences for discussion. Again, I was careful not to get into parental lecture mode. Instead, I would simply list real consequences. And unless the student could provide evidence that that consequence was not a likely threat, they were written down.

Then, without further ado, we went on to another solution and repeated the process. I typically found that having three viable solutions was all that was needed to start discussing which of the solutions provided the student with the best possible outcome.

The Pro vs. Con Decision-Making Process[9]:

- What are my choices?
- What are the DISADVANTAGES of each choice?
- What are the ADVANTAGES of each choice?
- Consider the options and possible consequences.
- Decide the best possible choice for YOU.

---

[9] Excerpted from Special Needs in the General Classroom, 500+ Teaching Strategies for Differentiating Instruction

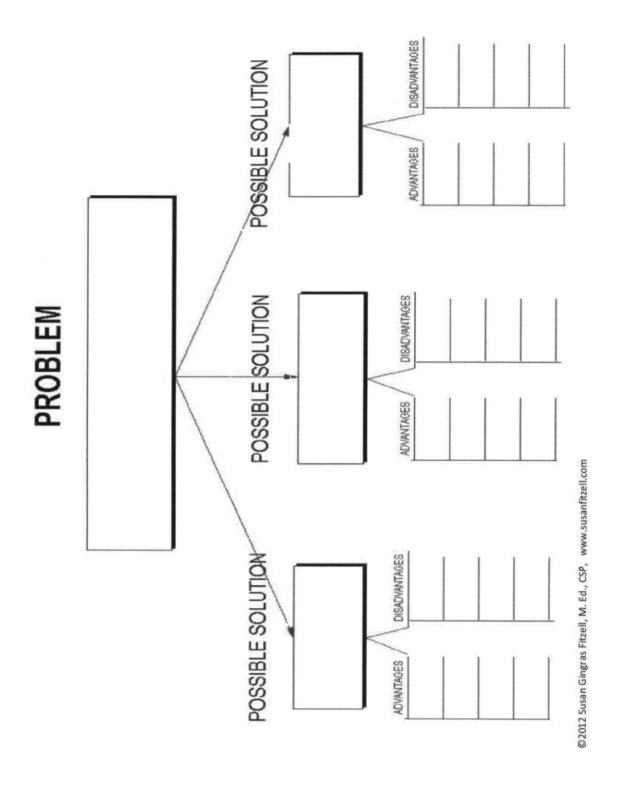

Behavioral Strategies for the Playground and Cafeteria

STRATEGY	EXPLANATION
State the expectation	Tell the student what to do and how you want them to do it.
Proximity	▪ Stand closer to the student's shoulder or arm while maintaining focus on the issue at hand. ▪ Lay your palm on the table or desk by the student's arm while maintaining focus on the student's behavior.
Gentle touch	Touch the student's shoulder or arm while maintaining focus on the issue. *Use ONLY if you feel this will de-escalate any conflict between you and the student.
Nonverbal cues	Smile, nod, or give a thumbs-up to reinforce appropriate behaviors.
Direct verbal cues	In a quiet and private manner, tell the student exactly how you want him or her to behave. End the statement by saying "Thank you." Step away from the student. During the interaction, act calm and dispassionate, regardless of how you actually feel.
Offer a choice	Offer the student a choice in which the options are incompatible with continuing the behavior. For example, when a student refuses to stop pushing or cutting in line, you could ask, "Do you want to stay where you are in line, or do you want to go to the end of the line? Make a good choice for yourself."

Playground Strategies

- Have different parts of the playground set out for games, quiet activities, playing with balls, etc. Frequently, conflict is triggered because children run into each other while playing, or children are excluded.
- Be vigilant watching over the students. The more staff that are actively supervising or engaging groups of students in games, the less likelihood of problems occurring.
- Deal with bullying and intimidation immediately. (Telling children to "Go and work it out" makes the victim feel invalidated, resentful, and powerless, and allows the bullying child to believe you do not care enough about it to take the time to deal with it. Some students bully simply because they can get away with it.)
- If you have a real and persistent problem with poor behavior on the playground, keep a camera handy and take pictures. Many times, just pointing the camera at the problem area will immediately stop problems. Students do not want a picture proving they were the cause of the problem.

Dealing with Tattling

The "It's not fair!" comment tends to peak among fourth graders. Children seem to notice every other child's infractions. Tattling is still common. Some children refuse to tattle because of social pressure, but they may "get even" instead. Help them become aware of their anger over an injustice. Teach them to stop and think before they react. What are the alternatives to tattling or retaliation?

Validate students' feelings. When a child tattles, often all they need is validation of their feelings. A question such as "How did that feel when Janie called you that name?" lets the child feel heard. To follow-up with empathy regarding their feelings and options for what they can do next usually leaves students feeling like they have been heard and they now have tools to handle the situation.

Teachers and parents often discourage tattling. By fifth grade, tattling is a major social taboo. The relief that upper elementary teachers and parents have from tattling holds hidden dangers. I asked a fifth grade class if they would tell if they knew someone had a gun in their backpack. To my astonishment, half of the class said they would not tell. They explained that it would be tattling. It is social suicide to tattle. In addition, telling might put them in danger.

I realized students needed to be taught that telling an authority when someone has a weapon, or someone is physically threatened, is following a safety rule. Kids are familiar with safety rules regarding fire, going with strangers, and riding bicycles. They have a certain amount of respect for these rules. They are accepted. Personal safety needs to be addressed in the same way. When we use authority to insure personal safety, it is not tattling, it is following a safety rule. The consequences of not telling must be made clear to the students.

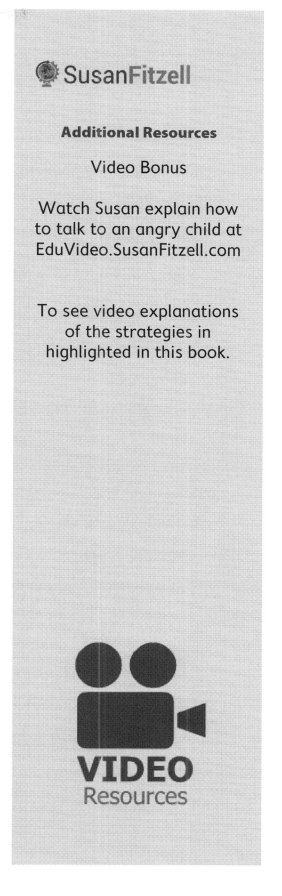

SusanFitzell

Additional Resources

Video Bonus

Watch Susan explain how to talk to an angry child at EduVideo.SusanFitzell.com

To see video explanations of the strategies in highlighted in this book.

VIDEO Resources

A TATTLE IS WHEN SOMEONE:

- Is trying to get attention for him or herself.
- Is trying to get someone else in trouble.
- Is trying to get his or her way.
- Can handle the problem by himself or herself.

REPORTING IS WHEN SOMEONE:

- Is trying to get help for a psychologically or physically harmful or dangerous situation.
- Is trying to get help for a scary occurrence or if someone needs protection.
- Needs help from an adult to solve the problem.
- Is trying to keep people safe.

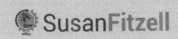

Additional Resources

This chapter provides several forms for you to use in your collaborative classrooms

Download printable and editable versions of the forms at **Bonus374**.susanfitzell.com

Also, you can download an 8x11 copy of the posters with accompanying lesson plans at the above link, also.

For a more complete and detailed support, get Susan's companion book in the series, *Special Needs in the General Classroom: 500+ Teaching Strategies* for *Differentiating Instruction, 3rd Edition*

Shop.SusanFitzell.com

Also, navigate to SusanFitzell.com for helpful articles.

For professional development options: SusanFitzell.com/Teachers/

Learned Helplessness

What Is Learned Helplessness?

Learned helplessness is a mindset that results from being conditioned through negative stimuli, to believe that you are powerless to control your destiny. This might include feeling stupid, destined for failure, incapable of doing things on your own. It may not affect every aspect of a person's life. It may only apply to school, or living in poverty, or the ability to escape a negative situation.

Learned helplessness is a concept that is considered to be a cognitive process where students perceive events which are controllable to be out of their control, and perhaps at times will see uncontrollable events as controllable (Peterson, Maier, & Seligman, 1993).

Learned helplessness can sometimes be a result of our doing too much for children when we're trying to help them. It's a common problem when working with students with special needs; adults struggle to know how much help is too much.

There have been research studies conducted to determine the effect of a paraprofessional–student relationship on student achievement and success(Giangreco, Edelman, Luiselli, & Macfarland, 1997; Russel, 2010). These studies concluded that a significant number of children who had paraprofessional support experienced learned helplessness. The term for the paraprofessional behavior that enabled learned helplessness is "hovering."

Hovering was used label behavior where too much is done for students by well-intentioned paraprofessionals. Sometimes parents require schools to provide support that may hinder the paraprofessional from providing students with opportunities to develop independence.

When youth depend on a paraprofessional to be successful in school, the youth then begins to feel like they're not in charge of themselves. They lose their sense of personal power: I don't have any power; I can't do that. I need help becomes their mantra.

Helping students who have learned helplessness to become confident, independent, and motivated to work on their own requires specific verbal scripts so as not to further solidify the students' sense of helplessness. The research says that if you try and help a student with learned helplessness and you do it wrong, you very well could make it worse, with all good intention. You really must know how to talk to children with learned helplessness (Miller & Seligman, 1975)

Be a Thought Detective

I was teaching high school and working with struggling learners. Many of my students were 'unmotivated,' felt defeated, believed they were stupid, etc., etc.

While researching solutions to counter negative thinking and Obsessive-Compulsive Disorder (OCD), I came across a book titled Freeing Your Child from Obsessive-Compulsive Disorder (Chansky, 2000). It is, by far, the most practical, common sense, solution book written in lay person's language on the topic of OCD. The author uses analogies, both verbal and visual, to help the reader understand how to approach the issue successfully. For example, one analogy compares OCD thoughts to junk mail.

My take-away from this book was not only relevant to people with OCD. It was relevant to everything we think and believe that feeds the thoughts in our brain. When youth appear to be unmotivated, ask them what they are thinking.

You might get responses like these: "Well, they're telling me... People don't like me," and "The teacher doesn't like me," or "I'm stupid," or "I'm not smart," or "I'm ugly."

A possible way to respond: "Okay, you know what? Those thoughts are like bullies. They are putting you down, telling you bad things about yourself. They are bullying thoughts. I want you to think about the bully in your brain, and you tell that bully that you don't want to listen to him anymore. You are in control of your thoughts."

It felt strange to consider using a strategy such as this with my students, because I feared there might be children who may think they're schizophrenic, or have multiple personalities, if I suggested such a thing. But on the other hand, I knew this really could work!

So, I tried the technique with some students, but instead of saying, "The bully in your brain." I said, "Be a mind detective. You've got thoughts going through your head. As a detective, determine: Are those thoughts negative? Are they positive? Are they telling you good things about yourself or bad things about yourself? What are they telling you? If they're telling you bad things about yourself, tell them to stop it. You are the one in control of your thoughts. You're the detective. When the detective tells you, 'They're saying these bad things,' you tell those thoughts 'No! No more.' Instead, choose thinking that is positive, that helps you to feel smart and powerful." Use positive self-talk. Positive thinking is significantly related to youth's engagement, self-confidence, imagination, and optimism in the learning process (Hong, Lin, & Lawrenz, 2012).

It sounds a little crazy, but again, it works! It's not very different from visualizing success. You're changing your thinking. You think it; you feel it; you do it. I've done a lot of research on this type of reprogramming our thoughts, gaining much from the works of Dr. Albert Ellis (Ellis, 2007).

Not everybody subscribes to that psychology, but I do because it works. There's a significant body of research behind it as well as hundreds of years of spiritual teaching out of the Eastern Philosophies. I realize that it is controversial in some religious circles and respect people's right to differ. I, however, cannot remain silent on something that has yielded concrete, positive results and thus freed people from emotional pain.

How to Curtail Learned Helplessness

- Encourage and reinforce a student's talents and abilities. Focus on what they can do rather than what they can't do. Say, "You're good at this." to things the student really is good at.
- When students make negative statements about themselves, help them reframe those statements to be positive. Instead of "I'm not good at math." Reframe to, "I can do math when I use these strategies."
- Help students figure out how they learn and be persistent in encouraging them to use those strategies and tools.
- Don't praise for praise's sake. Youth know when praise is empty. Telling a child they are the best ever, or so smart, or did a great job, when they know or feel that it is a lie is the worst thing we can do. Be very specific as to what a student has done well and make sure it's true. It is better to say, "You got three more done correctly than the last time." than to say, "Great job!"

- When a student states the equivalent of, "I only passed because I was lucky." Reframe that with, "You passed because you used your strategies and studied for that test."
- Teach students to be "thought detectives."
- Teach students to dispute automatic negative thoughts by gathering evidence that refutes those thoughts. Find evidence as to why those thoughts are wrong. It's important to not just tell the child they are wrong. They won't believe you. They need the evidence. Tell them what they do right, what they do well, what their talents are (Gordon & Gordon, 2006).
- Teach the child to set realistic goals for themselves.
- Teach the child strategies for distracting themselves from negative thinking.
- Implement a prompt hierarchy protocol.

Prompt Hierarchy

A prompt hierarchy(McDonnell, 1987) is a ladder of prompts that start with no prompt necessary because the student acts independently, to increasing levels of prompts ending with most dependent. Research has indicated that using a prompt hierarchy and weaning a student from higher need prompts to lesser need prompts can increase students' independence when implemented consistently and

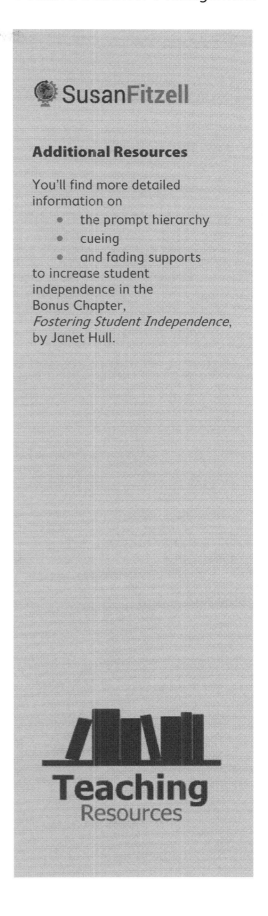

SusanFitzell

Additional Resources

You'll find more detailed information on
- the prompt hierarchy
- cueing
- and fading supports

to increase student independence in the Bonus Chapter, *Fostering Student Independence*, by Janet Hull.

Teaching Resources

101

with fidelity. In order to use this methodology effectively, educational staff must engage in professional development to learn the process and feel comfortable implementing it. (Austin, 2012)
Following is an example of a prompt hierarchy.

Pause - No Prompt

Allow the student time to respond or the opportunity to initiate communication

Indirect Nonverbal Prompt

Uses body language to cue the student to respond appropriately. Examples include: Facial expressions, gestures, or a combination that includes body language.

Indirect Verbal Prompt

Uses an open-ended question that indicates to the student that something is expected without being too specific.

Gestural Prompt

Uses gestures to point to an object, location, item on an assignment to cue the child to respond appropriately.

Model Prompt

Models appropriate response or behavior and waits for the student to imitate the response or behavior appropriately.

Physical Prompt

Provide hand-over-hand assistance to help the child with the task or expected behavior.

According to one study (Austin, 2012)where education professionals were trained to effectively use a prompt hierarchy to support students with significant cognitive disabilities, students were able to make progress in the general education curriculum. The study data indicated that instructional practices that included the use of a prompt hierarchy demonstrated positive findings in student achievement.

Non-confrontational Behavior Management Strategies

Using non-confrontational strategies for managing minor discipline problems or the early stages of potential problems can significantly reduce problems in the classroom. Depending on the strategies chosen, behavior may de-escalate or escalate. The goal of this section is to suggest strategies that de-escalate conflict or potential behavior problems.

Cueing Students to Redirect or Reinforce

Often, the best approach to managing student behavior is to quietly cue the student to stop their inappropriate behavior, return to task, or to continue positive behavior. Many times, simply making eye contact with a student and giving him or her, a certain look or gesture is all that is needed to communicate your message. Avoid doing things that may embarrass students.

Ways to cue students:
- Make eye contact.
- Use physical gestures (i.e., raising your hand in silence or enlisting a pre-taught signal known to the student).
- Tap or snap your fingers, cough, or clear your throat to get the student's attention and redirect.
- Facial expressions (i.e., smile).
- Body language (Be careful to be non-threatening. Avoid getting into the student's space).
- Create a simple stop/go cue card. One side is red and the other green. When you want a behavior to stop, show the red side. When you want a behavior to continue, show the green side. Use green to affirm or reinforce positive behavior.
- Create a pictorial behavior management cue card. This is especially helpful with students in the autistic spectrum.
- Use Social Stories Apps designed to visually cue students.
- Use available apps to help students make appropriate decisions.

Using a Visual Cue Card

Cue cards are an excellent instructional tool for teachers in the diverse classroom. Research has indicated that using cue cards with students can support their success both academically and behaviorally. Both students with and without academic challenges benefit from the use of cue cards in educational settings.

This cue card enables teachers to provide students with positive feedback or provide a needed redirection without stigmatizing or embarrassing the student. While using cue cards to redirect students to more positive behavior choices or to prompt recall of instruction, as a positive feedback tool, empowers students by recognizing their effort and success. (Conderman & Hedin, 2015)

Cue cards require modeling and practice prior to implementation to be effective. So, be sure to teach students how they will be used and what is expected in response. Whereas this cue card is ready-made and generic, they can be individualized to student needs.

Cue Card Instructions

1. Create your cue card to match redirection and praise you frequently state in class.
2. Stick the cue card on the top corner of each student's desk. (Laminate it, use shipping tape, etc. to make it sturdy.)
3. Rather than disturb the class with a verbal correction or embarrass a student with verbal praise, walk up to the student's desk and:
   a. Make eye contact.
   b. Point to the picture on the card that represents what you want to say.
   c. Walk away. (Do not say anything or engage in banter.)

Optional: You might also punch a hole in the laminated card and put it on a lanyard or keep it in your pocket. This is especially helpful if you cannot tape the cards to the students' desks.

Cue Card Example

Work Quietly 	**Get to work!** 	**Take out your pencil.** 
Open your book. 	**High five!** 	**You should be reading.** 
Show Respect. 	**You're doing Great!** 	**Thank you for doing the right thing.** THANK YOU!

Strategic Ignoring

Sometimes the best way to deal with student misbehavior is to ignore it.

When might it be best to ignore behavior?
- When the inappropriate behavior is unintentional or not likely to reoccur.
- When the student's goal is to get attention through misbehaving.
- When ignoring it will decrease misbehavior by not reinforcing it.
- When it is out of your area of jurisdiction.

When is it best not to ignore behavior?
- When there is physical danger or harm to yourself, others, or the student.
- When a student disrupts the classroom through inappropriate behavior.
- When a student violates class or school rules.
- When the behavior interferes with the student's or other students' learning.
- When the inappropriate behavior will incite other students to join in.
- When other students reinforce the misbehavior by snickering, laughing, and otherwise giving positive – or even negative – feedback.

Proximity Control

Stand or sit near a student who is having trouble. Also, circulating around the classroom will often help keep students on task because of your proximity to them. Students know you are aware of their behavior and will usually stop any inappropriate behavior quickly. This allows the classroom teacher to continue teaching without interrupting the lesson or the flow of the activity. As a caution, it's important not to reinforce negative behavior by calling attention to the student.

Communication Could Be the Solution!

Sometimes students become frustrated and violent because they are unable to verbally express what they need or want. Also, transitions are often difficult for students with special needs. It may be helpful to use pictures or photos as a communication tool. Pictures can be downloaded from the Internet from clipart sources or Google Images. There are also software programs like Mayer-Johnson's Boardmaker® specifically designed for this purpose.

Put Velcro® on the backs of the photos.
Put the other half of the Velcro on a piece of tag board or even an open file folder.

Arrange the pictures in the order of the student's daily schedule. Depending on the mental age or disability level of the student, you may need to help him or her with this at first. Say, "Now it's time for music," and hand-over-hand help him remove the picture of music and put it in a designated place (maybe an envelope that's attached to the board).

Also, have photos/pictures for the student to use to communicate his or her wishes and needs with you, such as drink, snack, bathroom, etc. In this way, the student can use the pictures to show you what he wants.

It might also be helpful to learn a few American Sign Language signs, such as stop, no, yes, bathroom, walk, etc., and then use them to reinforce your verbal cues.

Tips & Tools to Focus and Calm Students

Johnny walked through the classroom door late. I took one look and mused, "Whoa! He didn't take his meds today!" Before he made it to his seat in the front of the classroom, he had touched four other students, grabbed one girl's pen right out of her hand, kicked a backpack out of his way, shouted across the room at a friend, and dropped his books on his desk with a bang.

What was the rest of the period going to be like? Well, it was time to take out my bag of tricks and techniques. I handed Johnny a mandala and a bag of markers and said, "Johnny, I'm working on a new bulletin board and want to add some calming color. Would you please color one of these for me? Just work on it till we get started." Johnny happily obliged. I watched as he became physically calm. He was fine the rest of the period.

When faced with students having difficulty focusing, what can paraprofessionals do? Here's a list of suggestions to increase positive behavior, learning, and focus.

Environmental Strategies

- Seat distractible students surrounded by well-focused students.
- Provide study carrels or partitions to reduce visual distractions during seatwork or test-taking as appropriate. (This should be a student choice not a punishment.)
- Provide sound reducing headsets for students to minimize auditory distractions.
- During silent reading, consider allowing students to sit on the floor if they ask. Some students become amazingly focused when they carve out their own space on the floor or in a corner of the classroom.
- Silence the pen tapper with the sponge from a curler.
- Provide inexpensive craft rings threaded with beads to fidgeting students for calming.
- Stick a soft, fuzzy side of a strip of sticky backed Velcro to the underside of a desk for students who "pick" at things. Agree on a nonverbal cue to encourage the student to "pick" at the Velcro strip instead of other less desirable places.
- Keep mandalas and markers or colored pencils handy in the classroom for calming students. Coloring from outside in focuses attention, coloring from the inside out opens creativity.

- Have students who doodle, create doodles that illustrate their notes. Ask them to paraphrase what their doodles mean.
- Give an angry or over excited student some Silly Putty or TackyTac to knead as a calming strategy.

Physical Cues and Vocal Strategies

- Make use of nonverbal signals to cue student before transitions, or to stop all activity and focus on the teacher.
- Use physical proximity to help cue student to return to task.
- Vary tone of voice when presenting information. (If you can pull off a dramatic flair, it works well.)

Enlist Peer Supports

- Assign students 'Task Buddies' to help keep each other on task. Allow students to ask buddies for clarification on seatwork.
- Consider allowing students with Attention-deficit/hyperactivity disorder (ADHD) to "tutor" other students in areas of strength. This often brings out focused, caring behavior and encourages self-esteem.

Brain Gym®: A Wakeup Call to the Brain[10]

Brain Gym® is a series of exercises that enables the brain to work at its best. The techniques are a composite of many differing sciences based predominantly upon neurobiology. It has been found to facilitate learning in learning-disabled students. However, the results of using Brain Gym have proven to be highly effective for all learners. There is even evidence that Brain Gym can be used for psychological disorders as well.

Teachers will find these exercises enhance student performance before test-taking, but they also work before listening to lectures and studying. They also may relieve stress.

How does Brain Gym work? Carla Hannaford, Ph.D., neurophysiologist, states in "Smart Moves" that our bodies are very much a part of all our learning, and that learning is not an isolated "brain" function. Every nerve and cell is a network contributing to our intelligence and our learning capability. She states, "Movement activates the neural wiring throughout the body, making the whole body the instrument of learning." Hannaford states that "sensation" forms the basis of concepts from which "thinking" evolves.

Brain Gym exercises consider our bi-cameral brain. The brain has a left and a right hemisphere, each one doing certain distinct tasks. Generally, one side of our brain works more than the other, depending upon the tasks we are doing or how we have developed as human beings. If the two brains are working fully and sharing information across the corpus callosum, there is a balance of brain function. Without this balance, there is always going to be something that is not understood or remembered. Brain Gym assists in integrating the two brains, which gives us full capacity for problem-solving or learning.

We are also "electrical" beings and our brains' neurons work by electrical connections. Drinking water has been found to be the best thing we can do

---

[10] Adapted from an article by Ruth Trimble (trimble@hawaii.edu).

Much of the factual material for this section is taken from Smart Moves by Carla Hannaford, Ph.D. and Dr. Paul Dennison and his Educational Kinesiology (Edu-K) literature. Please cite these authors when using this material. There are qualified Brain Gym Instructors all over the country; a link to Brain Gym online resources is given in the appendix. Permission to use my data is given, but it constitutes only my opinion and limited practical experience and is not in any way intended to represent the official Brain Gym or Edu-K view, nor give permission to reproduce the detailed exercises designed by the other authors without citing them.

to facilitate the thinking process because of its capacity to conduct electricity and assist cell function. As Carla Hannaford says, "Water comprises more of the brain (with estimates of 90%) than of any other organ of the body." Thus, a simple drink of water before a test or before going to class can have a profound effect on our brains' readiness to work. Unfortunately, coffee or soda will have the opposite effect since these will upset the electrolytes in the brain. The exercises that you see here are designed to make us a whole-brain learner. Some simple but effective ways to wake up the brain and get it working instantly and optimally are listed on the following pages.

Before any of the following exercises, DRINK a glass of water.

"HOOK-UPS"

This works well for nerves before a test or special event such as making a speech. Any time there is nervousness or anxiety, this will bring a sense of calm.

1. Sit for this activity and cross the right leg over the left at the ankles.
2. Take your right wrist and cross it over the left wrist and link up the fingers so that the right wrist is on top.
3. Now bend the elbows out and gently turn the fingers in towards the body until they rest on the sternum (breast bone) in the center of the chest.
4. Stay in this position.
5. Touch your tongue to your palate.
6. Breathe in through your nose and out through your mouth in slow, deep, belly breaths.
7. Keep the ankles crossed and the wrists crossed and then breathe evenly in this position for a few minutes.
8. You will be noticeably calmer after that time.

Ruth Trimble states, "My student test scores have gone up because of Brain Gym. I have students achieving far higher scores than I have seen using the same screening and testing methods for the past six years. The ones who are doing Brain Gym are accomplishing so much more."

Mandalas as a Tool to Focus, Calm, and Get Creative

- Working from the center to the edge: Broadens attention
- Working from the edge to center: Focuses attention
- Relaxes the body
- Activates the right brain
- Visual prompt/structural map for writing feelings in a poem, song, or composition
- "Tilt the brain so language comes out differently" -Caryn Mirriam-Goldberg, author of *Write Where You Are* from Free Spirit Press

A source for mandalas can be found at http://www.mandali.com/.

Color Your Own Mandala[11]

Sample from Monique Mandali, *Everyone's Mandala Coloring Book*,
http://www.mandali.com/

---

[11] Sample from Monique Mandali, Everyone's Mandala Coloring Book, http://www.mandali.com/

Chapter 3 Review & Discussion Questions

Be a Positive Role Model

This section stresses the importance of treating students the way we would like to be treated and implores paraprofessionals and educators to model the desired behaviors in their actions. It also contrasts the concept of punishment versus discipline.

Reflect and Discuss

Consider a time you witnessed a punishment. Discuss with a partner, or self-reflect, how that punishment might have been changed into a discipline. Then, using any of the tools discussed in the chapter, create a plan to approach this issue in a collaborative manner.

Special Considerations for the Paraprofessional

This section highlights the restrictions placed on paraprofessionals to act with authority, and offers general behavior management tips in the form of a "do's and do not's" list.

Reflect and Discuss

In the previous activity, you changed a punishment into a discipline. Looking at the list in this chapter, which "Behaviors to Avoid" did you replace with "Techniques That Build Rapport & Foster Better Behavior"? Are there any other "Behaviors to Avoid" that you could replace?

Choice: Encourage Choice and Decision-Making

This section presents choice as a behavior management strategy and includes examples activities and scripts from every kind of activity a student may be involved in throughout the school day.

Take it to the Classroom - Practical Application

For Teachers – Rewrite a future lesson to include or increase student choice. (It may be a closed or open question format.) After you teach this lesson, write at least one paragraph reflecting on what worked, what didn't work, and how the lesson could be improved for future use.

<u>For Paraprofessionals</u> – Consider exchanges you have with students that are not listed in the example scripts. Create a script for offering choice in that situation. (It may be a closed or open question format.) When you encounter this situation again, employ the script you created. Afterwards, write at least one paragraph reflecting on what worked and what didn't work.

Behavioral Support Strategies for the Playground and Cafeteria

This section offers strategies to change student behavior in large group environments, such as on the playground or in the cafeteria.

Reflect and Discuss

Describe any situations beyond the playground or cafeteria where these strategies could be effective.

Non-confrontational Behavior Management

This section describes non-confrontational ways to easily and subtly reduce behavior problems.

Reflect and Discuss

- Which of the strategies from this chapter do you already use?
- Which strategies from this chapter would you like to incorporate?
- Outline an action plan for how you might begin using the strategies you chose to add.

Tips & Tools to Focus and Calm Students

This section offers strategies that the students can internalize in order to self-regulate their mood, attention, and behavior. Distracting or inappropriate behaviors are substituted for "teacher approved" alternatives.

Reflect and Discuss

Choose three strategies to implement in your lessons over the next week. After you have tried each strategy, write down your thoughts on what worked, what didn't work, and what could be improved. If age-appropriate, pass out a brief survey to the students to ask their opinions on the strategy.

℘ CHAPTER 4 ℘

Academic Support

This section includes strategies for one-to-one & small group instruction. These strategies can also be used with whole class instruction by paraprofessionals, as well as general and special education teachers.

Recent scientific research has confirmed that we all have different learning preferences and that we all learn best with strategies and techniques that honor our learning preferences. Brain research has taught us that we all process information in ways specific to our unique abilities. This section provides the reader with simple, proven tools to help students increase academic performance and make their learning experience more rewarding and productive. Tools provided will help students succeed at any grade level.

Understanding Special Needs

What Is Exceptionality Under Federal Law[12]?

Assessment and Federal Law

The Individuals with Disabilities Education Act (IDEA), Public Law 101-476, lists 13 separate categories of disabilities under which students may be eligible for special education and related services if they meet the requirement of being adversely affected.

These categories(U.S. Department of Education, 2017) are:

Autism

...means a developmental disability significantly affecting verbal and nonverbal communication and social interaction, generally evident before age three, that adversely affects a child's educational performance. Other characteristics often associated with autism are engaging in repetitive activities and stereotyped movements, resistance to environmental change or change in daily routines, and unusual responses to sensory experiences. The term autism does not apply if the child's educational performance is adversely affected primarily because the child has an emotional disturbance, as defined in #5 below.

A child who shows the characteristics of autism after age 3 could be diagnosed as having autism if the criteria above are satisfied.

Deaf-Blindness

...means concomitant [simultaneous] hearing and visual impairments, the combination of which causes such severe communication and other developmental and educational needs that they cannot be accommodated in special education programs solely for children with deafness or children with blindness.

---

[12] These category definitions are accurate as of 23/April/2017. These may change at any time. Please refer to ed.gov for current definitions and updated information

Deafness

...means a hearing impairment so severe that a child is impaired in processing linguistic information through hearing, with or without amplification, that adversely affects a child's educational performance.

Developmental Delay

...for children from birth to age three (under IDEA Part C) and children from ages three through nine (under IDEA Part B), the term developmental delay, as defined by each state, means a delay in one or more of the following areas: physical development; cognitive development; communication; social or emotional development; or adaptive [behavioral] development.

Emotional Disturbance

...means a condition exhibiting one or more of the following characteristics over a long period of time and to a marked degree that adversely affects a child's educational performance:

- An inability to learn that cannot be explained by intellectual, sensory, or health factors.
- An inability to build or maintain satisfactory interpersonal relationships with peers and teachers.
- Inappropriate types of behavior or feelings under normal circumstances.
- A general pervasive mood of unhappiness or depression.
- A tendency to develop physical symptoms or fears associated with personal or school problems.

The term includes schizophrenia. The term does not apply to children who are socially maladjusted, unless it is determined that they have an emotional disturbance.

Hearing Impairment

...means an impairment in hearing, whether permanent or fluctuating, that adversely affects a child's educational performance but is not included under the definition of "deafness."

Intellectual Disability

...means significantly subaverage general intellectual functioning, existing concurrently [at the same time] with deficits in adaptive behavior and manifested during the developmental period, that adversely affects a child's educational performance.

Editor's Note, February 2011: "Intellectual Disability" is a new term in IDEA. Until October 2010, the law used the term "mental retardation." In October 2010, Rosa's Law was signed into law by President Obama. Rosa's Law changed the term to be used in future to "intellectual disability." The definition of the term itself did not change and is what has just been shown above.

Multiple Disabilities

...means concomitant [simultaneous] impairments (such as intellectual disability-blindness, intellectual disability-orthopedic impairment, etc.), the combination of which causes such severe educational needs that they cannot be accommodated in a special education program solely for one of the impairments. The term does not include deaf-blindness.

Orthopedic Impairment

...means a severe orthopedic impairment that adversely affects a child's educational performance. The term includes impairments caused by a congenital anomaly, impairments caused by disease (e.g., poliomyelitis, bone tuberculosis), and impairments from other causes (e.g., cerebral palsy, amputations, and fractures or burns that cause contractures).

Other Health Impairment

...means having limited strength, vitality, or alertness, including a heightened alertness to environmental stimuli, that results in limited alertness with respect to the educational environment, that—

- is due to chronic or acute health problems such as asthma, attention deficit disorder or attention deficit hyperactivity disorder, diabetes, epilepsy, a heart condition, hemophilia, lead poisoning, leukemia, nephritis, rheumatic fever, sickle cell anemia, and Tourette syndrome; and
- adversely affects a child's educational performance.

Specific Learning Disability

...means a disorder in one or more of the basic psychological processes involved in understanding or in using language, spoken, or written, that may manifest itself in the imperfect ability to listen, think, speak, read, write, spell, or to do mathematical calculations. The term includes such conditions as perceptual disabilities, brain injury, minimal brain dysfunction, dyslexia, and developmental aphasia. The term does not include learning problems that are primarily the result of visual, hearing, or motor disabilities; of intellectual disability; of emotional disturbance; or of environmental, cultural, or economic disadvantage.

Speech or Language Impairment

...means a communication disorder such as stuttering, impaired articulation, a language impairment, or a voice impairment that adversely affects a child's educational performance.

Traumatic Brain Injury

...means an acquired injury to the brain caused by an external physical force, resulting in total or partial functional disability or psychosocial impairment, or both, that adversely affects a child's educational performance. The term applies to open or closed head injuries resulting in impairments in one or more areas, such as cognition; language; memory; attention; reasoning; abstract thinking; judgment; problem-solving; sensory, perceptual, and motor abilities; psychosocial behavior; physical functions; information processing; and speech.

The term does not apply to brain injuries that are congenital or degenerative, or to brain injuries induced by birth trauma.

Visual Impairment Including Blindness

...means an impairment in vision that, even with correction, adversely affects a child's educational performance. The term includes both partial sight and blindness.

Considering the Meaning of "Adversely Affects"

You may have noticed that the phrase "adversely affects educational performance" appears in most of the disability definitions. This does not mean, however, that a child must be failing in school to receive special education and related services. According to IDEA, states must make a free appropriate public education available to "any individual child with a disability who needs special education and related services, even if the child has not failed or been retained in a course or grade, and is advancing from grade to grade." [§300.101(c)(1)]

Related Terminology (Rogers, n.d.)

- Chronologically age-appropriate: A standard by which students' activities may be evaluated. Instruction and materials should be directed at the student's actual age, rather than to the interests and tastes of younger students.

- Cognitive: A term which refers to reasoning or intellectual capacity.

- Disability: A physical, sensory, cognitive, or affective impairment that causes the student to need special education. NOTE: There are significant differences in the definitions of disability in IDEA and Section 504.

- Due process: In general, due process includes the elements of notice, opportunity to be heard, and to defend ones' self. With regard to IDEA, due process refers to a specific set of procedures described in 23 IAC Part 226. With regard to Section 504, procedures are less clearly specified. With regard to student discipline matters, the amount of process that is due is largely dependent upon the degree of jeopardy involved.

- Fine motor: Functions that require tiny muscle movements. For example, writing or typing would require fine motor movement.

- Functional curriculum: A curriculum focused on practical life skills and usually taught in community-based settings with concrete materials that are a regular part of everyday life. The purpose of this type of instruction is to maximize the student's generalization to real life use of his/her skills.

- Gross motor: Functions which require large muscle movements. For example, walking or jumping would require gross motor movement.

- Heterogeneous grouping: An educational practice in which students of diverse abilities are placed within the same instructional groups. This practice is usually helpful in the integration of students with disabilities.

- Homogeneous grouping: An educational practice in which students of similar abilities are placed within the same instructional groups. This practice usually serves as a barrier to the integration of students with disabilities.

- IEP - Individualized Education Plan: The document developed at an IEP meeting which sets the standard by which subsequent special education services are usually determined appropriate.

- IEP meeting: A gathering required at least annually under IDEA in which an IEP is developed for a student receiving special education.

- IDEA: Law that modifies and extends the Education for All Handicapped Students Act (EHA).
- LRE: Least restrictive environment. A requirement of IDEA.
- Occupational therapy: A special education-related service which is usually focused upon the development of a student's fine motor skills and/or the identification of adapted ways of accomplishing activities of daily living, when a student's disabilities preclude doing those tasks in typical ways (e.g. modifying clothing so a person without arms can dress himself/herself).
- Permanent record: A brief document upon which essential information is entered and preserved. The contents of the permanent record are specified in the Illinois Student Records Act.
- Placement: The setting in which the special education service is delivered to the student. It must be derived from the student's IEP.
- Section 504: Provision of the Rehabilitation Act of 1973 which prohibits recipients of federal funds from discrimination against persons with disabilities.
- Supplementary aids and services: Accommodations which could permit a student to profit from instruction in the least restrictive environment. They are required under IDEA.
- Total communication: An instructional strategy in which paraprofessionals or teachers instruct students with severe hearing loss both by speaking to them and by using sign language. The theory is that if the students can learn to speak, then the stimulation is being presented. Even if they do not learn to speak, they will still be provided with a language-rich environment.
- Visual-motor: Coordination of what is seen with an action. For example, one uses visual-motor coordination when catching a ball.

Theory of Multiple Intelligences

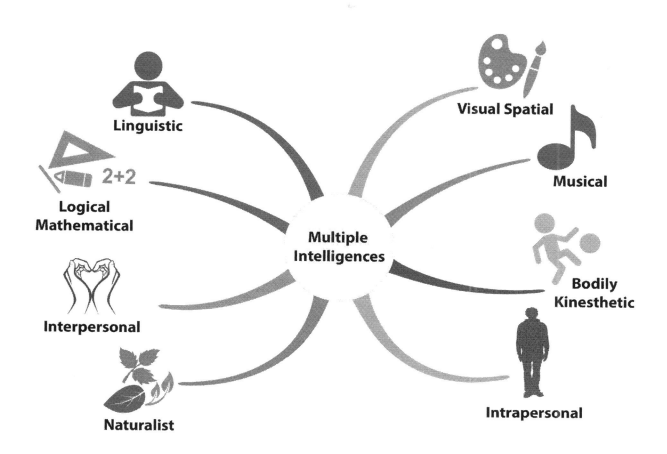

Psychologist Howard Gardner identified the following distinct types of intelligence in his book, *Frames of Mind*. Per his theory, all people possess eight distinct sets of capabilities. Gardner emphasizes that these capabilities/intelligences work together, not in isolation. The intelligences, including his newest finding, the Naturalist, are:

Linguistic: Young people with this kind of intelligence use words effectively, either orally or in writing. They enjoy writing, reading, telling stories, or doing crossword puzzles.

Logical-Mathematical: Children have the capacity to use numbers effectively and to reason well. They are interested in patterns, categories, and relationships. They are drawn to arithmetic problems, strategy games, and experiments.

Bodily Kinesthetic: Children with this capability are experts in using their whole body to express ideas and feelings. They are good with their hands. These kids process knowledge through bodily sensations. They are often athletic, dancers, or good at crafts such as sewing or woodworking.

Spatial: These young people think in images and pictures. They may be fascinated with mazes or jigsaw puzzles, or spend free time drawing, building with construction sets, or inventing.

Musical: Musical students have the capacity to perceive, discriminate, transform, and express musical forms. They often spend time singing or drumming to themselves. They are usually quite aware of sounds others may miss. These kids are often discriminating listeners.

Interpersonal: These students can perceive and make distinctions in the moods, intentions, motivations, and feelings of other people. They are often leaders among their peers, who are good at communicating and responding to others' feelings.

Intrapersonal: These students are insightful and self-aware. They can adapt to their environment based on their understanding of themselves. These students may be shy. They are very aware of their own emotions, strengths, and limitations, and have the capacity for self-discipline.

Naturalist: The core of the Naturalist intelligence is the human ability to recognize plants, animals, and other parts of the natural environment, like clouds or rocks. These students can identify and classify patterns in nature. These students are sensitive to changes in the weather or are adept at distinguishing nuances between large quantities of similar objects.

Existentialist: Students who learn in the context of where humankind stands in the "big picture" of existence. They ask, "Why are we here?" and "What is our role in the world?" This intelligence is seen in the discipline of philosophy.

Allow students to use the following lists to figure out how they learn best. Some students may need to have the lists read to them.

Someone who is Verbal/Linguistic

- Tells tall tales, jokes, and stories
- Has a good memory
- Enjoys word games
- Enjoys reading and writing
- Has a good vocabulary for his/her age
- Has good verbal communication
- Enjoys crossword puzzles
- Appreciates nonsense rhymes, puns, tongue twisters, etc.
- Spells words accurately (or if preschool, spells using sounds that is advanced for age)

Someone who is Logical-Mathematical

- Asks questions about how things work
- Enjoys math activities
- Enjoys playing chess, checkers, or other strategy games
- Enjoys logic puzzles or brain teasers
- Interested in patterns, categories, and relationships
- Likes doing and creating experiments
- Does arithmetic problems in his or her head quickly (or if preschool, math concepts are advanced for age)
- Has a good sense of cause and effect

Someone who is Bodily Kinesthetic

- Excels in one or more sports or physical arts
- Moves, twitches, taps, or fidgets while seated for a long time
- Enjoys taking things apart and putting them back together
- Touches new objects
- Enjoys running, jumping, or wrestling
- Expresses him or herself dramatically
- Enjoys modeling clay and finger painting
- Good with his or her hands
- Cleverly mimics other people's gestures or mannerisms

Someone who is Musical Rhythmic

- Recognizes off-key music
- Remembers melodies
- Plays a musical instrument or sings in a choir
- Speaks or moves rhythmically
- Taps rhythmically as he or she works
- Is sensitive to environmental noise
- Responds favorably to music
- Sings songs that he or she has learned outside of the classroom
- Is a discriminating listener
- Creates his or her own songs and melodies

Someone who is Intrapersonal

- Displays a sense of independence or a strong will
- Has a realistic sense of his or her strengths
- Has a good sense of self-direction
- Prefers working alone to working with others; may be shy
- Learns from his or her failures and successes
- Is insightful and self-aware
- Adapts well to his or her environment
- Aware of own emotions, strengths, and limitations
- Is self-disciplined
- Marches to the beat of different drummer in his/her style of living and learning

Someone who is Spatial

- Daydreams more than peers
- Enjoys art activities, puzzles, and mazes
- Likes visual presentations
- Understands more from pictures than words while reading
- Doodles on paper
- Loves construction sets: Legos, K'nex, Capsela, etc.
- Frequently, inventing things
- Draws things that are advanced for age
- Reads maps, charts, and diagrams more easily than text (or if preschool, enjoys looking at more than text)

Someone who is Interpersonal

- Enjoys socializing with peers
- Acts as a natural leader
- Gives advice to friends who have problems
- Seems to be street-smart
- Belongs to clubs, committees, or other organizations
- Likes to play games with other kids
- Has one or more close friends
- Shows concern for others
- Perceives and makes distinctions in people's moods, intentions, and motivations
- Good at responding to other people's feelings

Someone who is Naturalist

- Enjoys labeling and identifying nature
- Sensitive to changes in weather
- Good at distinguishing among cars, sneakers, and jewelry, etc.

Someone Who Is Existentialist (Possible 9th Intelligence):

- Learns in the context of where humankind stands in the "big picture" of existence
- Asks "Why are we here?" and "What is our role in the world?"
- This intelligence is seen in the discipline of philosophy

Strategies for Multiple Intelligences & Differentiation

Suggestions for Assignments (Based on Multiple Intelligences)

For Verbal/Linguistic Learners

- ☐ Allow options for students to choose from when assigning projects, research, study, and practice
- ☐ Create radio or TV advertisements (see History Project example)
- ☐ Debate current events
- ☐ Create crossword puzzles
- ☐ Teach the class the steps to....
- ☐ Write a script

For Logical-Mathematical Learners

- ☐ Compare and contrast ideas
- ☐ Create a timeline
- ☐ Classify concepts/objects/materials
- ☐ Read or design maps
- ☐ Create a computer program
- ☐ Create story problems for....
- ☐ Design and conduct an experiment on....
- ☐ Use a Venn diagram to explain....
- ☐ Teach using technology

For Bodily Kinesthetic Learners

- ☐ Create hands-on projects
- ☐ Conduct hands-on experiments
- ☐ Create human sculptures to illustrate situations
- ☐ Design something that requires applying math concepts
- ☐ Re-enact great moments from history
- ☐ Study body language from different cultural situations
- ☐ Make task or puzzle cards for....

For Musical Rhythmic Learners

- ☐ Create "raps" (key dates, math, poems)
- ☐ Identify social issues through lyrics
- ☐ Analyze different historical periods through their music
- ☐ Make up sounds for different math operations or processes
- ☐ Use music to enhance the learning of....
- ☐ Write a new ending to a song so that it explains....

For Intrapersonal Learners

- ☐ Keep a journal to demonstrate learning
- ☐ Analyze historical personalities
- ☐ Imagine self as character in history, a scientist, or mathematician and describe what you imagine demonstrating your knowledge

For Visual-Spatial Learners

- ☐ Make visual organizer or memory model of the material being learned (give copies to other students in the class)
- ☐ Graph the results of a survey or results from a course of study
- ☐ Create posters or flyers
- ☐ Create collages
- ☐ Draw maps
- ☐ Study the art of a culture
- ☐ Color-code the process of....

For Interpersonal Learners

- ☐ Analyze a story
- ☐ Review material/concepts/books orally
- ☐ Discuss/debate controversial issues
- ☐ Find relationships between objects, cultures, situations
- ☐ Role-play a conversation with an important historical figure
- ☐ Solve complex word problems in a group
- ☐ Peer tutor the subject being learned

For Naturalist Learners

- ☐ Sort and classify content in relation to the natural world
- ☐ Interact with nature through field trips
- ☐ Encourage learning in natural surroundings
- ☐ Categorize facts about....

Brain-Based Research & Implications for Learning

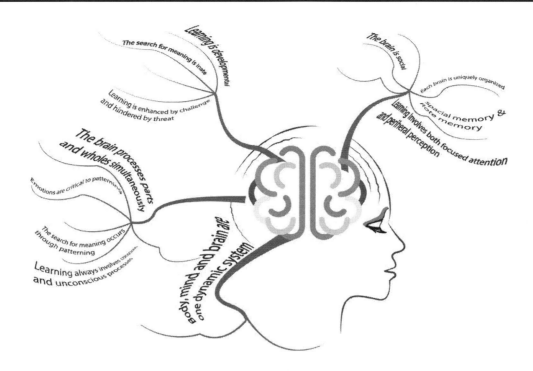

Questions and Answers About Brain Research

The brain reacts to shape, color, sound, texture, and light, yet teachers in the upper grades through high school still tend to teach through lecture — verbal linguistic methods. Focusing on language based teaching nourishes the left side of the brain but ignores the right side, which is dedicated to creative thinking.

Who Is Doing Brain Research?

Studies on the brain depend on research generated from the fields of Molecular Biology, psychoneuropharmacology, neurobiology, and neuroscience. The tools of exploration improve annually with advancements in computer technology and more precise methods of observing actual brain functioning as opposed to postmortem studies.

How Do Scientists Research the Brain?

Scientists use electrodes and amplifiers to map the brain's electrical activity. These studies are illuminating the sophisticated communication system established between brain cells. Neurobiologists study the communication between brain chemicals and the rest of the body's nervous system.

Neuroanatomists use electronic microscopes to trace the neural pathways from deep within the brain all the way down to the big toes.(Alivisatos et al., 2012; Kriegeskorte, Goebel, & Bandettini, 2006; Salmelin & Baillet, 2009)

Does Brain Research Prescribe Proven Methods of Instructions?

Neuroscience lends credibility to many principles of good instruction, but this field does not purport to prescribe specific ways to teach or a new and improved curriculum. Much of the work on the brain is applied from laboratory studies using mice, kittens, primates, fruit flies, samples of fetal tissue, and others. Educators must use caution when choosing teaching methods: don't throw the baby out with the bathwater (in comes brain-based techniques, out goes everything else, or vice versa). Yet there is significant evidence to warrant encouraging those charged with rearing and educating young children to carefully tend to the brain's intrinsic need for meaningful experience, nurturance, and safety.

Learning and Brain Chemicals

Have you heard about the brain chemicals that foster learning and the flight or fight brain chemicals that stop learning? How does thinking positively help you to learn? It releases chemicals in your brain that support learning. It releases dopamine and epinephrine in the right amounts.

I used to think positive thinking was 'fluff'. I'm not a touchy-feely kind of person, so I pooh-poohed it. But the research shows that, biologically, positive thinking literally builds neural connections in your brain. You're firing off neurons and dendrites that are releasing dopamine (Shohamy & Adcock, 2010), noradrenaline and other brain chemicals which, in fact, support successful learning.

Negative self-talk releases too much cortisol, which is a stress hormone, and increased levels of cortisol impair working memory (Oei, Everaerd, Elzinga, van Well, & Bermond, 2006). This is not psychological. It's biological.

If I'm stressed, I'm releasing cortisol. Cortisol is your fight-or-flight chemical (Jansen, Nguyen, Karpitskiy, Mettenleiter, & Loewy, 1995) and it's there to protect you from that raging tiger that's coming towards you. Your students and your children don't know the difference between a raging tiger coming towards them and a piece of paper that's a test.

The calmer I am going into a test, the calmer I am going into a learning situation, the better off I am and the more likely that brain chemicals are working in my favor, rather than against me by causing short-term memory impairment.

12 Brain-Based Learning Principles

Renate Nummela Caine and Geoffrey Caine (Caine, Caine, McClintic, Klimek, & Costa, n.d.)identified basic patterns of how human beings learn. They call these the Twelve Principles of Brain-Based Learning. (Org, Caine, & Caine, n.d.) To summarize, there are at least twelve principles of brain-compatible learning that have emerged from brain research.

- Uniqueness – Every single brain is totally unique and becomes more unique as we age.
- A threatening environment or stress can alter and impair learning and even kill brain cells.
- Emotions are critical to learning – They drive our attention, health, learning, meaning, and memory.
- Information is stored and retrieved through multiple memory and neural pathways that are continually being formed.
- All learning is mind-body – Movement, foods, attention cycles, drugs, and chemicals all have powerful modulating effects on learning.
- The brain is a complex and adaptive system – Effective change involves the entire complex system.
- Patterns and programs drive our understanding – Intelligence is the ability to elicit and to construct useful patterns.
- The brain is meaning-driven – Meaning is more important to the brain than information.
- Learning is often rich and non-conscious – We process both parts and wholes simultaneously and are affected a great deal by peripheral influences.
- The brain develops better in concert with other brains – Intelligence is valued in the context of the society in which we live.
- The brain develops with various stages of readiness.
- Enrichment – The brain can grow new connections at any age. Complex, challenging experiences with feedback are best. Cognitive skills develop better with music and motor skills.

Strategies for Brain-Based Learning

☐ Dim the lights if possible, or use blue, green, pink, or full-spectrum lighting in the classroom (Cooper, 1999).

☐ Play classical music – Classical music connects with the brain, enabling students to learn better and to relax. Music should have less than 60 beats per minute.(Jausovec, Jausovec, & Gerlic, 2006) (Jausovec et al., 2006).

☐ Give students choices (Kohn, 1993).

☐ Use color to categorize, highlight important text, group like items, etc. (Hayes, Heit, & Rotello, 2014).

☐ Alternate the color of bullets on digital screens (e.g. Interactive white boards), whiteboards, and chalkboards.

☐ Use colored borders for information that you want students to notice or remember.

☐ Border printed spelling words to accentuate the "shape" of the word.

☐ Allow opportunity for expressing emotions and listening to others' feelings.

☐ Take more stretch breaks and, when possible, incorporate brain-stimulating movement.

☐ Drink water – The brain needs hydration. Students need at least 40 ounces of water a day.

☐ Relate learning to real world experiences – Make it meaningful.

☐ Reduce stress in the classroom – Stress hinders learning. Students perform best when they do not feel they are competing with each other for the highest grades (Oei, Everaerd, Elzinga, Van Well, & Bermond, 2006; Romain & Verdick, 2000; Vedhara, Hyde, Gilchrist, Tytherleigh, & Plummer, 2000).

☐ Use the "Power of Two" (work partners) for pulse learning.

☐ Use learner-imposed deadlines.

☐ Use graphic organizers, group, and classify, and teach through telling stories!

☐ Create visual cues – draw pictures with stick figures or use clip art to illustrate important events and concepts. See Figures 1 and 2 by Sean McCready for examples.

Setting up the Environment for Learning

Paraprofessionals do not always have control over the work environment. When it is possible to influence the learning environment the following considerations and strategies are recommended.

Provide a Comfortable Place to Work Without Distractions.

Calm restless students with wordless music at 60 beats per minute or less.

- Helps with attention issues and sensory processing
- Supports organized body movement
- Assists active engagement of the learner
- Increases both alpha and beta brain waves which are associated with a quiet, alert state that is receptive for learning
- Helps to provide structure for organized thinking, e.g. writing reports or papers, activities that involve planning

Suggestions:
- Native American Flute
- Peruvian Mantra
- Mozart for Learning (Caution: Some classical is too rambunctious. The key is 60 beats per minute or less)
- Enya
- Yanni
- Mellow jazz

Typically, any music without words that cannot be sung (and therefore distracting) will work

Choose Where to Sit (Or Stand) for Independent Activities

Traditionally, students sit at desks in the classroom. We know, however, that some students will spend all their time, whether consciously or unconsciously, looking for ways to get away from their desk. This poses a behavior challenge for teachers and paraprofessionals and isn't the optimum learning environment for some students.

Teachers often assign specific seats to students to control class behavior and maintain focus and attention. However, would it be reasonable to allow students to choose where to sit during specific activities? What if students were required to sit in assigned seats for direct teaching, yet could sit where they want for independent work? Of course, the classroom teacher needs to be on board when providing this option.

Even in high school, students might prefer to sit on the floor to work or collaborate. Why not allow them to sit where their bodies are more comfortable? Class rules still need to be reiterated and enforced. If they sit with their friend and they're off-task, then they may need an adult to make the choice of where to sit for them. Be certain that they understand this would be a logical consequence of their choice.

What if they ask to stand? I had students who struggled to sit in the classroom and I realized one day that if I allowed them to stand and work off the bookcase, they were more focused and their behavior significantly improved. When my son was little, he'd eat better if he could stand at the dining room table. It also minimized trips to the hospital after he fell out of his chair.

And as for myself, I can't sit to focus. I create a standing station in my office with a lap desk on top of the desk, and in a hotel room by placing an upside-down drawer on the desk. I put my laptop on top of the drawer.

Consider helping students to figure out how and where they learn best and encourage them to use what they know about their how they learn to succeed.

Cueing Strategies that Foster Learning

The Correct Way to Help a Student

How do we help our youth without doing too much for them?

For example: You've got a student who's taking a test and is stuck on a question.

Tell Them What They've Done Correctly

Find something right about what they've done. They don't need to hear what they did wrong. Instead, tell them what they did correctly, so that they feel a measure of personal power and capability.

Always Start with What They Did Right

This strategy is an excellent communication strategy when dealing with anybody, whether in the workplace, in your family, or at school.

My personality style is: one who critiques first, and my business manager is: one who appreciates first, so if I critique first, he often perceives my critique as hurtful. I've had 14 years of working with him to learn how to appreciate first.

I've had to learn this same approach when communicating with my son. He's the only 'feeling' type personality in my house, and is quite sensitive. Certain personalities really need you to appreciate first, to find out what's right first, and not to go right to the critique. It may seem like it's more efficient to go directly to the point, however, it can be the worst thing you can do and a strong de-motivator.

If it's your personality style to critique first, train yourself to appreciate first. Practice the skill, it will pay off immensely.

Teach the Next Step and Leave!

After you've told them what they've done right, then tell them the next step. Don't get into long explanations; just tell them the next step: The next step is this. It may be counter-intuitive. It may seem illogical to not tell them why. But a contributor to learned helplessness is that learning becomes overwhelming (Mikulincer, 1995).

If they're getting it wrong and they're frustrated, and we try to take the time to go through this long explanation about why it's wrong, what to do next and how to do it, that youth is on sensory overload.

The conversation might sound like this: "Yes, you got that right. You got the notes down just beautifully, there. Here's what you do next. Okay. You're on your own."

Walk Away – Leave and Don't Look Back!

This is the hardest thing to do!

Now, they might say, "But... but can you...?"

No! They may try to guilt you into not leaving them, but no; you go! You walk away. Resist the urge to take care of them! Resist the urge to do it for them! Resist the urge to give in! Resist.

SusanFitzell

Additional Resources

Video Bonus

Navigate to
EduVideo.SusanFitzell.com

To see video explanations of the strategies in highlighted in this book.

VIDEO Resources

Personally, I can relate to this. I realize I learn the same way. If I'm stuck, don't give me a detailed explanation. Just tell me what to do to get to the next step. In that moment of 'stuckness' that's what I need. Teach me the explanation later when there's more time, I'm less frustrated and I'm calm. Or, let me learn on my own in my own time. If you try to give me a long, detailed explanation I'll quickly reach overload. I'm a visual learner, so telling me isn't going to help anyway. Draw me a picture.

Mimicking vs. Being Forced to Think

I have about a dozen children in my martial arts class. When teaching them their martial arts forms, we do a continuous series of moves. I stand in front of them and do the forms while they follow along behind me. They stand behind me and they just do beautifully.

I thought, "These kids are good!" When I first started teaching kung fu, I couldn't understand how we could do the same moves for weeks with students following along perfectly. Then on a review day, I'd say, "Okay, Johnny, step up to the front and show me 'Eight Chain Punch.'" He couldn't do it. One day, I realized that my students had been copying me! Children are excellent mimics. While we were in class, they had been watching me and copying the moves. Then they went home and couldn't remember the moves to practice on their own.

What I've learned teaching martial arts is this: Sometimes you've got to show them a little and walk away! That's how my martial arts instructors taught me. As a new martial arts student, I was frustrated at the expectation that I could be shown a move and two minutes later be expected to practice it on my own. I know what happens in my brain – I forget and must dig deep to recall what I was shown.

The reality is that to internalize new material, you must make yourself think about what you are supposed to do. You might get it wrong, but at least you're getting your brain and those neural connections working, and that gets it into your memory, a little bit at a time.

If we help youth through the whole process, they won't know how to do it on their own afterwards. It's hard as a parent or teacher, especially when working with a student who struggles, to walk away and let them sort the learning out. But we must let them practice, so that they learn and remember.

How Much Can We Help Them on a Test?

Guidelines for cueing students is to give them hint without telling them too much.

CUE:

Point out what is 'right' in student's response. Then take the student back to the 'instructional moment' so they can visualize the lesson. The visualization may cue the student's memory.

ASSOCIATE:

Give a verbal prompt to trigger student's memory for connections or associations that will facilitate recall. For example:
- Question: "What is the symbol for Mercury?"
- Student: "I don't know."
- Cue: "Hug (Hg) a thermometer and it'll get hot!"

CLUE:

Give a verbal or nonverbal hint such as a key word, beginning sound, etc. to prod student's memory.
- Question: "What is the symbol for Mercury?"
- Student: "Mc?"
- Cue: "No; it starts with an 'H'."

CLARIFY:

Ask a probing question to encourage students to elaborate and enhance their answer with more details and less imprecision.
- Question: "Should society have the right to tell you how to behave on your own time?"
- Student: "No. It causes other problems."
- Cue: "What kind of problems? Can you give examples?"

PROBE:

Ask question(s) that guide a student towards making a more complete or appropriate response.
- Question: "What is the cause of our ozone depletion?"
- Student: "Chlorofluorocarbons."
- Cue: "How do you know chlorofluorocarbons are destroying the ozone layer?"

Strategies to Assist with Learning

Many students with learning disabilities struggle with memory deficits. Primarily, they forget information they need to do well on tests or to do the higher-level thinking required for problem-solving, analysis, and synthesis. For example, if students can't remember basic math facts, even if they have a calculator at their disposal, they will take longer to complete a test, thereby impacting their test scores.

Working memory space(Nelson Cowan, 2010) for these students is being used up with basic calculations rather than higher-level thinking skills. Students who struggle to remember the details of a story can't draw inferences from those details because they can't remember the sequence of events or what happened at various parts of the story.

Remembering the details and foundation of what is being taught is critical to comprehending, applying, and analyzing what is being taught. An intervention strategy to differentiate instruction for students struggling to remember information in the classroom is to use short-term memory strategies.

Limit Information

The brain can only hold seven pieces of information at a time in short-term memory. What this means is that if we teach for 20 minutes and we've given students more than seven things to remember, it's too much. If we put up a slide and there are more than seven things on it, it's probably too much for the brain.

The only way we can sometimes get away with more than seven facts is if they are written in a large font (Hughes & Wilkins, 2000), or if we 'chunk' related information by color. The brain can process information quickly from a PowerPoint presentation if we've chunked it with color. So, if we have eight or nine things, we might be able to use color to make it more like seven if some of those things go together.

For example, five facts about short-term memory might be green, five facts about working memory could be brown, and five facts about long-term memory could be black. We chunk related information by color.

Paraphrase Immediately

Another strategy to enhance short-term memory so information isn't "gone" in two seconds is to have a student paraphrase what we just taught. For example, after you've taught something important, ask a volunteer to paraphrase that information for the class. Most likely, your students will not relate the information in the same words you used, which will be novel to the brain. This strategy only takes seconds to do, yet it lets your students hear the information again, in a different way, with a different voice. The brain likes novelty and will remember the information better.

Paraphrase One Hour Later

Ask your students to paraphrase information that was shared earlier in the day. When they take something, you taught an hour ago and bring it back into play, it returns to short-term memory and is then pushed into working memory. Using this paraphrasing strategy in your classrooms will help students to remember what you are teaching.

Nonlinguistic Representation

This book, and the principles discussed within it, are about scientifically supported, classroom tested, best practice teaching. No matter what theories, programs, or vernacular we are currently using in education, some information must be remembered for later recall. This is a simple fact; both of life and of learning.

The strategies outlined in this chapter offer a variety of solutions for helping our students store the information we offer them, and successfully recall that information when they need it again. Also, strategies such as metacognitive mind mapping and attaching learning to real life application support higher-level thinking including comprehension, analysis, and evaluation.

Most of these strategies include Nonlinguistic Representation components. Academic research has consistently indicated that creating nonlinguistic representations requires students to think about content in new ways. Students will need to create a representation of new information that does not rely on text or verbal language. Representations need to be meaningful and related to the content. Nonlinguistic Representation is more than "just drawing pictures." It is drawing images or maps that represent the information being conveyed in a meaningful way.(Marzano, 2010)

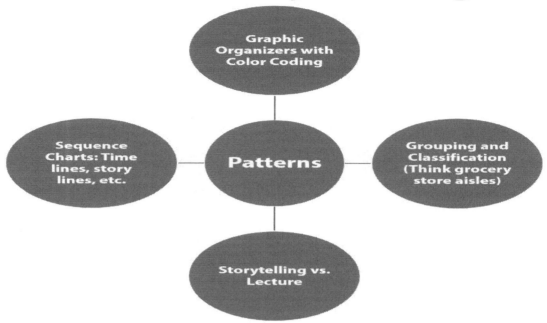

Mind Mapping/Graphic Roadmaps/Visual Organizers

I started using mind mapping after reading *I Can See You Naked: A Fearless Guide to Making Great Presentations* by Ron Hoff. My first presentation was drawn out like a colorful board game with a route to follow, arrows, and picture images of what I was going to do. I remember thinking how much easier it was to use than index cards with a text script written on them. It also was much less restricting. I did not feel tied to reading the cards. Rather, I looked at the picture and went from memory. It saved me from the plight of many presenters: that of being tied to a script. The technique worked so well for me that I started expanding the idea into my teaching efforts.

> *As I read selections from English texts to my students, I drew the events out on paper in map and graphic format.*

I would often interject silly ditties and exclamations of passion into the in effort to make what I was reading to them stick out in their memory. Given my students were at the 'cool' age of 'teen' they would often look at me and say, "You are crazy!" My pat answer was always, "Yes, I am, but you'll remember this because of it." Moreover, they did.

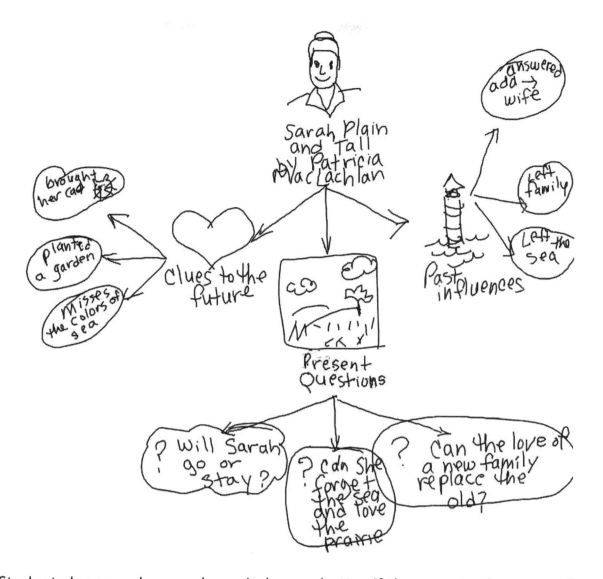

Students learn and remember mind maps better if they create them out of their own mental images and patterns. One can define a mind map as follows: A mind map consists of a central word or concept, around which you draw 5 to 10 main ideas that relate to that central word. You then take each of those 'new' words and again draw 5 to 10 main ideas that relate to each of those words. You can find more information on mind maps on Wikipedia: http://en.wikipedia.org/wiki/Mind_map.

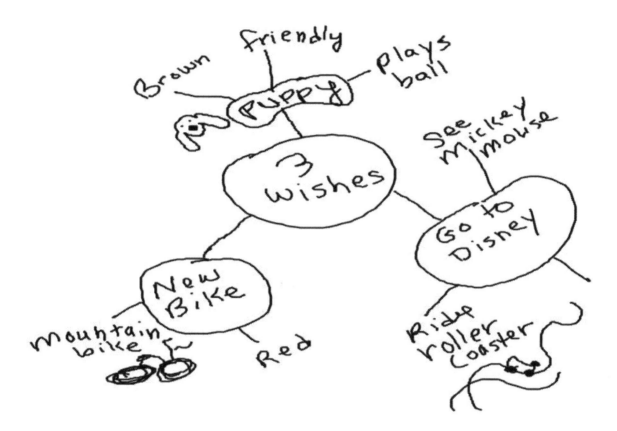

When students make spelling errors at this phase of the creative process, note them, but let them go. Correcting students' spelling while they are creating will cause them to clutter their working memory with rules and not allow enough "space" for coming up with ideas. So, correct the difference between 'add' and 'ad' later.

Mnemonic Devices[13]

Mnemonic. n. A device, such as a formula or rhyme, used as an aid in remembering.

Mnemonics, or the science or art of aiding memory, is an ancient concept. Many people rely on mnemonic devices to help remember what they have learned or need to recall, from grocery lists to people's names to kings and queens or the presidents. What works for one person may not work for another(Mastropieri & Scruggs, 1998).

The following memory devices may help improve retention of information. Some examples of mnemonics:
- I AM A PERSON: The four Oceans (Indian, Arctic, Atlantic, and Pacific)
- HOMES: Huron, Ontario, Michigan, Erie, and Superior: The Great Lakes in North America

The best are those made up by the student, as they are meaningful to him/her.

Associations

Developing associations is a familiar strategy used to recall information by connecting it to other, more familiar pieces of information. For example, memorizing a sequence of seemingly random digits is easy when that number series is your birth date or street address. Developing associations is also a helpful way to remember new information.

Rhyming

Rhymes and jingles are powerful memory devices (Claussen M.H., Thaut, Claussen, Thaut, & Claussen; Thaut;, 1997). Just think how often you have used the rhyme "Thirty days has September..." to recall the number of days within a month.

To use the rhyme technique, all you must do is make up a rhyme to remember what you want your students to remember. It's fun! If you have students who are musically inclined, encourage them to make up songs to

---

[13] Adapted from the work of Michael DiSpezio, author of *Critical Thinking Puzzles* (Sterling, 1996) for Scientific American Frontiers.

help them remember long pieces of important information, then share them with the rest of the class.

Examples:

- 30 days has September
April, June, and November

- In 1492, Columbus sailed the ocean blue

- In 1903, the Wright brothers flew free
First successful flight

- I before E except after C
And when saying "A" as in Neighbor or Weigh
And weird is weird

Chunking

The brain can only hold three to four pieces of information, or "chunks", in short-term memory at a time. (N Cowan, 2001; Farrington, 2011; Oberauer & Hein, 2012) To keep a lot of information in short-term memory, we naturally break it up into more manageable parts by chunking it in a meaningful way.

When reciting a telephone or Social Security number, most people break it up into three chunks. For example, the first and second chunks of a phone number consist of three digits, and the third chunk contains four digits. Here's a series of numbers that, at first glance, appears meaningless:

8005663712

However, once you realize it's a toll-free phone number, chunking the numbers and creating a mnemonic makes the series easier to remember. The mnemonic I created to remember this number – my old '800' number – draws on my background and experience. Someone else trying to remember the same information would come up with a mnemonic that's meaningful to them in order to remember this number.

800-566-3712

My mnemonic for this phone number is: *Five watched while big bully 7 blocked 3 from taking his place with friends 1 and 2.*

Chunking is also an excellent strategy for remembering how to spell words.

An example of chunking follows:

man ℰⅼⅼ **ver**

Other examples of chunked spelling words:
ALBU QUER QUE
RE NUMER ATION
PENN SYLVAN IA
CZ ECHO SLO VAKIA
LEU KE MIA
RECE IVE
Chunking information and associating it with information we've already learned, whether it's numbers, math formulas, spelling vocabulary, or anything else, helps us remember it more easily.

Acronyms

An acronym is a word formed from the first letter(s) of each word in a phrase or name. For example, **LASER** stands for Light Amplification by Stimulated Emission of Radiation. Other familiar acronyms are **RADAR**, **REM** sleep, **SCUBA**, **SONAR**, **NASA**, and **ZIP** code. You can make up acronyms to help students remember information. Think of an acronym as a "fun" word or phrase in which each letter stands for the first letter of the item to be recalled.

Acrostics

An acrostic is similar to an acronym, but it takes the first letters of a series of words, lines, or verses to form a memorable phrase. Sometimes the phrase is nonsense, which may help your students remember it! Here are two: Kings Play Cards On Fat Green Stools or King Philip Came Over For Grandma's Soup.

Taxonomy

King Philip Came Over For Grandma's Soup.
Kingdom Phylum Class Order Family Genus Species

© AIMHI Ed Programs

Each word in the acrostic stands for the biological classification hierarchy: Kingdom, Phylum, Class, Order, Family, Genus, and Species. By creating a visual image to go along with the phrase, we're incorporating multiple brain-based principles for memorization. When students make up their own acrostics and draw images to illustrate them, this is an especially powerful tool for memorization.

Strategy to Remember Sequences

Use adding machine tape to create a visual storyline, timeline, or sequence to be memorized.

As your students are reading a textbook or story, have them draw pictures of the important information (characters, historical figures, places, events, etc.) in the order the information is presented on adding machine tape.

For example, say your class is studying Native American practices. When students read about how the Lakota determined directions, they draw a picture representing the concept on the tape. Next the chapter describes what types of information were recorded, such as position of the sun, the moon, neighbor sites, and more. The class draws and labels that information in the same sequence/order that it is described in the textbook. See the following examples:

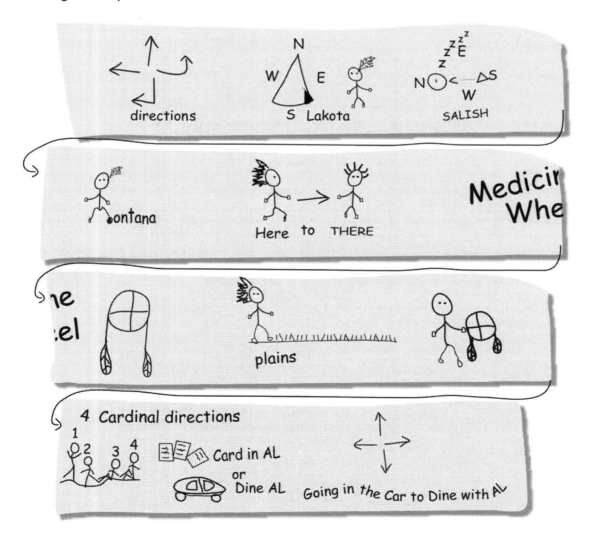

Now your students have a "timeline" or "story line" in sequential order of the practice as described in the textbook or story. This technique can be especially helpful in English and Literature classes; although the novels taught in high school classes rarely come with illustrations, students can draw the storyline in sequential order to remember key characters and the order in which the events in the story take place.

For example, in reading Albert Camus's *The Plague*, students may draw a sequence like the one below. They can make the storyline as detailed as they'd like — or as detailed as they need to remember the key events, triggering the memory when it's time for exams.

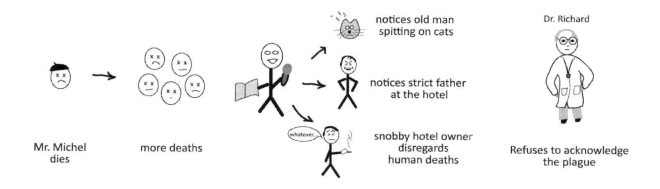

Mr. Michel dies | more deaths | notices old man spitting on cats | notices strict father at the hotel | snobby hotel owner disregards human deaths | Dr. Richard | Refuses to acknowledge the plague

This visual memory tool will help students remember the information in the order that it happened.

Draw It So You'll Know It

Contributed by 7th Grade Science Class, Kennedy Middle School, Waltham MA

Teachers often present information verbally and linguistically. However, many of our students are visual learners. A substantial amount of our brain power is devoted to visual processing. When we add a visual component, a drawing compon
ent, to what we are teaching, student recall increases.

When students are reading, or reviewing previously read material...
- Have them draw pictures of what they are reading.
- Have them illustrate their notes with drawings that represent the concepts and facts in their notes.

Although represented in black and white here, this drawing – as well as many of the illustrations throughout this book – was originally created in color.

Color and Memory

Simply put, we remember what we see in color better than what we see in black and white. (Hall & Sidio-Hall, 1994; Wong, 2011)), we remember colors first and content next. Colors affect us on both psychological and physiological levels.

Here are just a few ways you can use color in the classroom:
- Use colored handouts
- Add color to overheads

- Print notes and alternate two colors for each individual point
- Hang colorful posters to reinforce concepts being taught
- Provide colorful visuals

According to the research, color communicates more effectively than black and white. How much more effectively? Here's what the research says:

- Color visuals increase willingness to read by up to 80 percent.[14]
- Using color can increase motivation and participation by up to 80 percent.[11]
- Color enhances learning and improves retention by more than 75 percent.[15]
- Color accounts for 60 percent of the acceptance or rejection of an object and is a critical factor in the success of any visual experience.[16]

The Meaning of Color

Color	
Red	• An engaging and emotive color which can stimulate hunger or excite and disturb the individual
Yellow	• The first color distinguished by the brain
Blue	• Calms a tense person and increases feelings of well-being
Green	• A calming color, like blue
Brown	• Promotes a sense of security and relaxation and reduces fatigue

Three Card Match: Review

Materials

    Index cards

- Choose three of the following card colors: pink, green, blue, yellow, or white.

---

[14]Green, Ronald E. "The Persuasive Properties of Color." *Marketing Communications*, October 1984.
[15] Loyola University School of Business, Chicago, IL., as reported in Hewlett-Packard's *Advisor*, June 1999.
[16] Walker, Morton. *The Power of Color*. New York: Avery Publishing Group, 1991.

- If you only have white cards or white paper, color-code the cards. For example:
- Put a yellow dot or stripe on the word cards.
- Put a green dot or stripe on the picture cards.
- Put a pink dot or stripe on the definition cards...and so on and so forth. Pictures
- Of the item being reviewed
- Or related to the concept being reviewed
- Or mnemonic pictures to form an association

Instructions

- Break down what students must memorize into three related concepts, facts, pictures, meanings, etc.
- Each card should contain one 'item.' (See example below.)
- Label the back of each card in a set with a number, so children can turn the card over and self-correct.

For example:

- The word elephant, the picture of the elephant and the definition of the elephant would all be numbered #1 on the back.
- The word zebra, the picture of the zebra and the definition of the zebra would all be numbered #2, etc.

el·e·phant

An enormous mammal with a very long nose called a trunk.

Options for use:

- Students can match the cards on their own as a review in the resource room or classroom. If they have their own sets, they may use them at home to study.
- Students can pair up to match the cards. This is an excellent peer tutoring activity.

Visual Or Mnemonic	Word	Definition
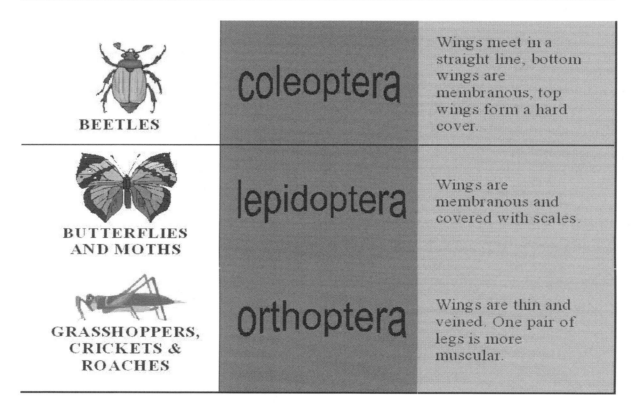	Folium of Descartes	x^3 + y^3 == 3x*y
BEETLES	coleoptera	Wings meet in a straight line, bottom wings are membranous, top wings form a hard cover.
BUTTERFLIES AND MOTHS	lepidoptera	Wings are membranous and covered with scales.
GRASSHOPPERS, CRICKETS & ROACHES	orthoptera	Wings are thin and veined. One pair of legs is more muscular.

The Fitzpell Method of Studying Spelling Words

Option 1: Use phonics rules to determine which letters should be in a **stand-out color**.

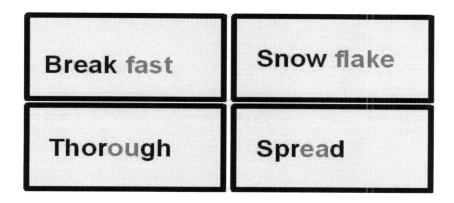

Option 2: Pre-test
Use pre-test errors to determine which letters should be in a **stand-out color**.
Theory: Make the corrected mistake in spelling stand-out so the mistake is not repeated.

Whenever possible, add clip art pictures to 'visualize' the word.
1. Use bright color markers with good contrast to differentiate.
2. Add any other symbols, sound cues, etc. to make the spelling word more memorable.
3. PRINT the words on INDEX CARDS.
4. Practice by running through the cards two to three times each day for the four days before the spelling test. Put aside the cards that need more study. Cards that can be spelled quickly can be pulled out of the daily second and third run.

Option 3: Put the key words in the question and the key words in the answer in a different color than the rest of the text.

Good luck!
You should see a significant improvement in spelling test grades.

Mind & Body Connection

Strategies

Use movement to enhance memory.

- Act out vocabulary words.
- Come up with a gesture to represent key people, places, or things.
- Use sign language.
- If you can take students to the gym, make a game out of spelling a word then shooting a basket. It doesn't matter what rules you make up. What is important is the movement, fun, and challenge in the activity.
- If you like football, soccer, or any other sports better, use that sport as a foundation. Make your own rules. As long as spelling, etc. is part of the game rules, it will be effective.
- Hop & Chunk Spelling – Students spell out a word and jump between each chunk of the word.
- Break a word into spelling "chunks" and hop while spelling each chunk. E.g.: Maneuver = Man (hop) eu (hop) ver (hop).

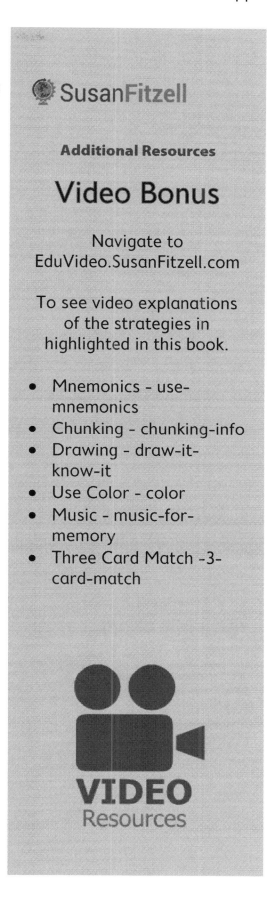

SusanFitzell

Additional Resources

Video Bonus

Navigate to
EduVideo.SusanFitzell.com

To see video explanations of the strategies in highlighted in this book.

- Mnemonics - use-mnemonics
- Chunking - chunking-info
- Drawing - draw-it-know-it
- Use Color - color
- Music - music-for-memory
- Three Card Match -3-card-match

VIDEO Resources

Make it Meaningful

Bring Emotion into the Lesson

We remember things that evoke our emotion. Advertisers use this knowledge effectively. When we can bring drama into the classroom, we will see increased learning. I will never forget the Western Civilization professor that I had in college and the excitement and passion she demonstrated for her subject. I hated history all through high school. Suddenly, I found myself enjoying a history class. Between my use of mnemonics and the teacher's drama,

enthusiasm, and ability to relate what she taught to the real world (including our future), I learned and loved it! Thanks Ms. Civitello!

- Make it a story
- Read with dramatization
- Use a gripping picture

Whenever possible, introduce concepts with pictures that evoke emotions. Many times, we focus on the printed word in texts and make minimal use of the photos. Artwork and drama reach the heart. Use it whenever possible to hook your students into the lesson.

Note: Use Photos as Tools for Brain-Based Learning and Multiple Intelligences.

Strategy for Getting "Un-Stuck" While Writing: Clustering

I can't even begin to count the amount of times that students would sit in study lab with pen or pencil staring at a paper unable to write that required introductory sentence. It seemed as if the phrase introductory sentence triggered writers block. I understood this on a personal level because I have never been able to write by beginning with the introductory sentence. Interestingly, when I have taken writing courses geared towards becoming an author, one of the first directions given is to just start writing, anywhere, anytime, anyplace. Just start writing. Never have I heard instructors say, "Okay, everyone write the introductory sentence of your book." Linear thinkers may work well with an outline and by starting at the beginning. Random thinkers, however, need to write ideas down as soon as they think them. Ideas must be captured before they are lost.

The clustering activity detailed on the following pages helps students who are struggling to write an essay, as well as young adults filling out college applications.

Clustering Activity Step One

- If your students must write a paper, instruct them to draw a big circle on a piece of paper.
- Put the topic of the paper in the center of the circle. Note: If there is more than one topic, you might have more than one circle. For example, writing about three wishes will require three circles: one for each wish.
- Instruct the students to write any thoughts, ideas, and feelings about the topic in the circle. Students can also ask questions about the topic or draw pictures of ideas.
- Do not worry about spelling, grammar, sentences, etc. at this point. The purpose is to get the ideas out. Worry about writing rules later.

Clustering: Free up Working Memory

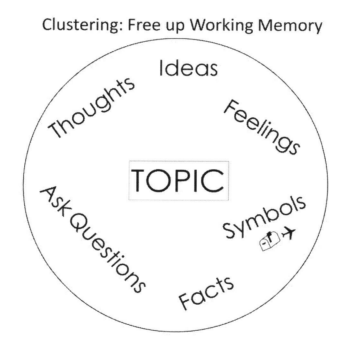

Make this circle BIG; at least the size of an 8" X 8" piece of paper.

- After students "create" in the circle, allow them to share what they have written with a partner.

Clustering- Step Two

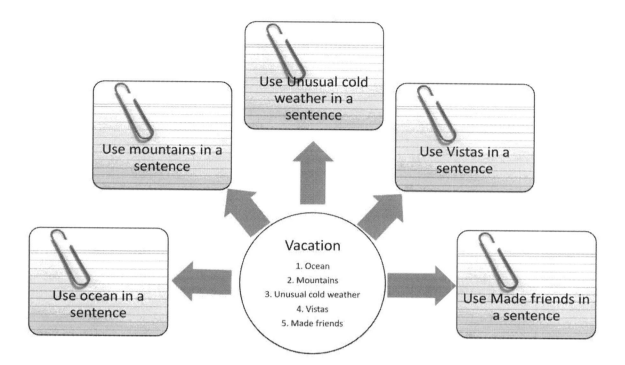

- Instruct students to take the "best" words and ideas from inside their circle and use each word in a sentence.
- This is the topic sentence for the paragraphs they will write.
- Write the sentences on strips of lined notepaper or lined sticky notes.

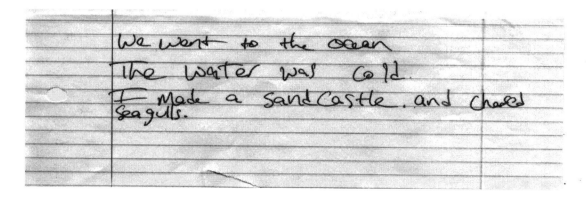

Clustering- Step Three

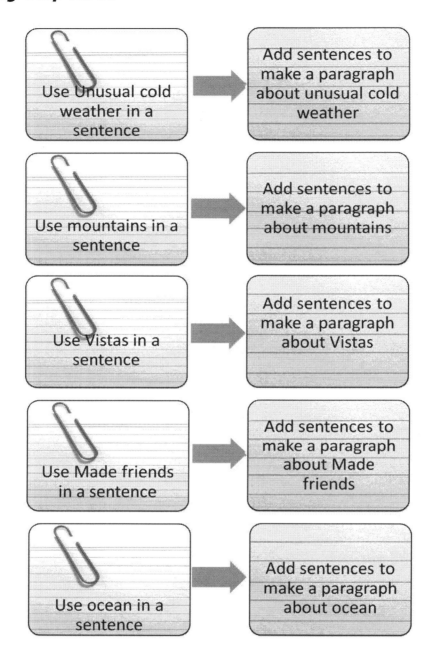

- Now, take each sentence and add some more sentences about the topic sentence on that strip of paper.
- Try to write two or three more sentences about the topic sentence.

*NOTE: Do not worry about spelling, grammar, or punctuation at this point in the exercise. Worrying about the rules makes it more difficult to be creative.

Clustering- Step Four

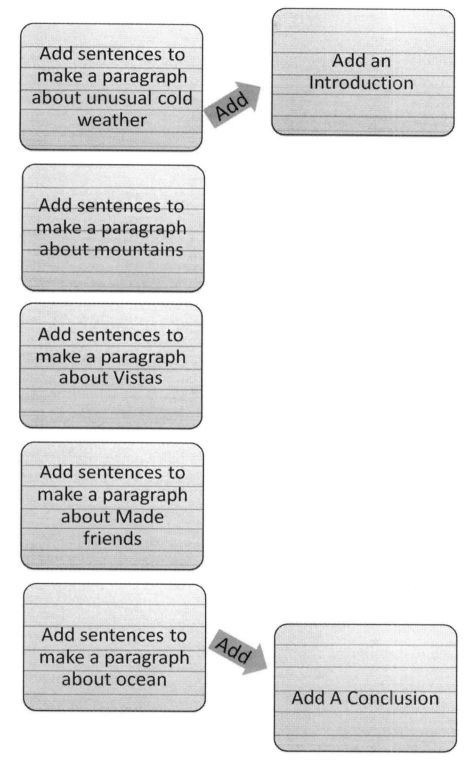

- Next, add an introduction and conclusion on separate strips of lined paper.

Clustering- Step Five

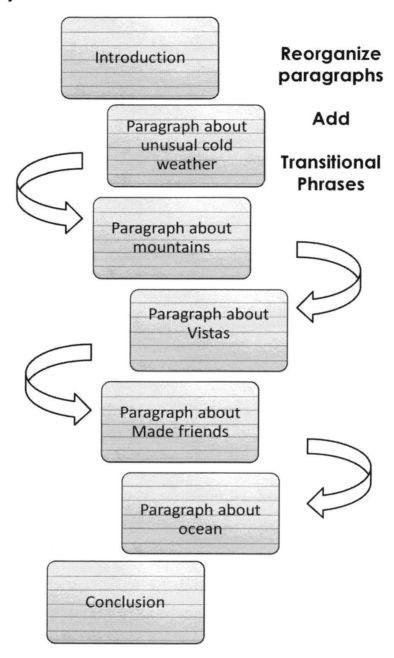

- Next, move the strips of paper around so that the paper is in the best order and makes the most sense.
- This process allows the writer to start anywhere in the paper. It frees up creative thinking and encourages the process to start. Organizing the paper after paragraphs are written is easy.
- Tape all the strips on one or two big pieces of paper.
- Add transition words to make the paragraphs flow together.

Transition Words:

To Add:
And, again, and then, besides, equally important, finally, further, furthermore, nor, too, next, lastly, what's more, moreover, in addition, first (second, etc.)

To Compare:
Whereas, but, yet, on the other hand, however, nevertheless, on the other hand, on the contrary, by comparison, where, compared to, up against, balanced against, but, although, conversely, meanwhile, after all, in contrast, although this may be true

To Prove:
Because, for, since, for the same reason, obviously, evidently, furthermore, moreover, besides, indeed, in fact, in addition, in any case, that is

To Show Exception:
Yet, still, however, nevertheless, in spite of, despite, of course, once in a while, sometimes

To Show Time:
Immediately, thereafter, soon, after a few hours, finally, then, later, previously, formerly, first (second, etc.), next, and then

To Repeat:
In brief, as I have said, as I have noted, as has been noted

To Emphasize:
Definitely, extremely, obviously, in fact, indeed, in any case, absolutely, positively, naturally, surprisingly, always, forever, perennially, eternally, never, emphatically, unquestionably, without a doubt, certainly, undeniably, without reservation

To Show Sequence:
First, second, third, and so forth. A, B, C, and so forth. Next, then, following this, at this time, now, at this point, after, afterward, subsequently, finally, consequently, previously, before this, simultaneously, concurrently, thus, therefore, hence, next, and then, soon

To Give an Example:
For example, for instance, in this case, in another case, on this occasion, in this situation, take the case of, to demonstrate, to illustrate, as an illustration

To Summarize or Conclude:
In brief, on the whole, summing up, to conclude, in conclusion, as I have shown, as I have said, hence, therefore, accordingly, thus, as a result, consequently, on the whole

Clustering- Step Six

Introduction

Paragraph about Made friends

Paragraph about mountains

Paragraph about Vistas

Paragraph about ocean

Paragraph about unusual cold weather

Conclusion

Rewrite or type into one continuous draft on full sheets of paper.

Hand in draft for the teacher to correct.

If the teacher is not correcting a draft, parents may be able to help with this step.

This is the time when the student uses the rules and makes sure that spelling, grammar, and punctuation are correct.

Clustering- Step Seven

Student writes
final draft
incorporating
teacher
corrections,
feedback and edits

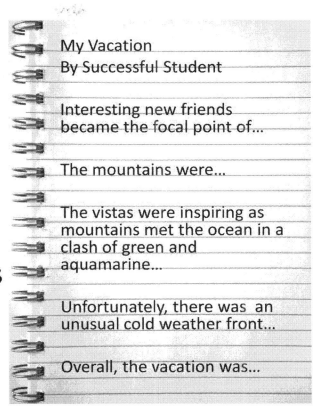

My Vacation
By Successful Student

Interesting new friends
became the focal point of...

The mountains were...

The vistas were inspiring as
mountains met the ocean in a
clash of green and
aquamarine...

Unfortunately, there was an
unusual cold weather front...

Overall, the vacation was...

Music as a Memory Strategy

Do you remember the lyrics to songs you listened to when you were a teenager? Can you still remember the words to songs you learned when you were in elementary school? Maybe these songs helped you to learn content such as grammar (Grammar Rock) or math (Multiplication Rock). Songs, chants, and raps help students memorize information and provide a hook for retrieving that information easily later. (Claussen M.H. et al., 1997; Gfeller, 1983; Wallace, 1994)

You and your students can create and perform songs for learning by substituting the lyrics in karaoke songs with the information that must be memorized. Take a nursery rhyme or folk song and substitute the words with the facts students must learn. Whether you purchase ready-made music for learning or create your own, this memorization technique helps students retain what they have learned and provides them with a way to access that information in long-term memory.

Rap it! Chant it! Clap it!

Here are some examples:
Quadratic Equation to the Tune of "Pop! Goes the Weasel."

> x e-quals neg-a-tive b
> plus or minus the squaaaare root
> of b squared minus fouuur a c
> all over twooo a

Helping Verbs to the Tune of "Mary Had a Little Lamb"

> Is, are, was, were, am, be, been
> Have, has, had
> Do, did, does
> May, might, mu-ust,
> Can, will, shall,
> Could, would, should, being

Math Tip for Visual-Spatial

Difficulties

Particularly in learning math, disorganized workspaces clutter up working memory because students are too busy trying to make order out of chaos to focus on the actual math problem. Helping students organize their workspace is one of the best ways we can help students with math (Levine, 2003). Following are some simple solutions to organizing math instruction for students.

- Write down the steps to the problem before solving it.
- Avoid mental arithmetic; use a scratch pad or scrap paper.
- If students become overwhelmed by looking at the entire test page, have them use blank paper to cover up

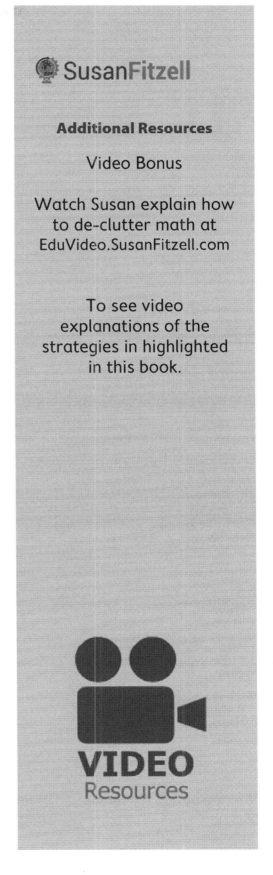

SusanFitzell

Additional Resources

Video Bonus

Watch Susan explain how to de-clutter math at EduVideo.SusanFitzell.com

To see video explanations of the strategies in highlighted in this book.

VIDEO Resources

173

everything but the problem they are working on so they don't become stressed. When they do not have to look at everything at once, they can focus more productively.

When students are working to organize their workspace, or trying to decipher their work, they are using up working memory on organization rather than the math process. These strategies allow them to focus on the math.

The following strategy allows them to focus on the math instead of using mind space organizing the numbers:

Unlined paper is the worst place to do math, especially for children with visual-spatial problems. Give them lined paper sideways and have them write the numbers in the columns.

Paraprofessionals can easily support students using this strategy even if working with materials that are not set up this way. Have students switch to lined paper turned sideways or use grid/graph paper.
Consider laminating dark lined grid paper. Students place the laminated grid under worksheets and workbook pages to line up their math!

For young children, use wide lined paper or paper with a large grid.

To download your own printable Line Sheets, go to www.printablepaper.net

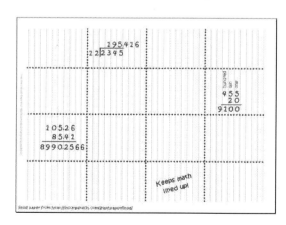

From Memorization and Test-Taking Strategies for the Differentiated, Inclusive and RTI Classroom (S. G. Fitzell, 2010)

Individual White Boards

Use individual sized white boards to encourage participation:

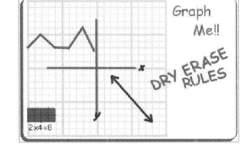

a   Every student has a:
   1) Whiteboard
   2) Dry-erase marker or wipe-off crayon
   3) Little kid sock (for wiping and storing marker or crayon)
b   The paraprofessional asks a question.
c   Students write answers on white boards.
d   After fair amount of time, teacher asks students to hold up boards.
e   The paraprofessional can see how ALL students are doing in one look across the room.

It stops blurters and allows those that need processing time to finally get it! (Rowe, 1986)

Note-Taking Strategies

Cut and Paste Notes Using Mind Maps and Charts

Consider the graphic organizer on the following page and the different ways it can be used to differentiate:

1. Whenever you are presenting a "process," show the process visually in a process map. This will help the students to visually see what you are teaching and will enhance memory of the process.
2. Give students a process map or a graphic organizer with blank boxes and choose option a, b, or c below.
   a. Have students fill in the key words as you teach about the topic.
   b. Give students a grid of the key words, a glue stick, and scissors. Have them cut out the words.
      i. Then as you <u>teach</u> the lesson, instruct students to move the words to the correct box and paste them down.
      ii. Then as you <u>review</u> the lesson, instruct students to move the words to the correct box and paste them down.
      iii. <u>Power of Two</u>: Instruct students to work together to decide where the words go on the map and move the words to the correct box. Teacher might review student's answers and, when correct, instruct them to paste them down.
   c. The graphic organizer can be used as a quiz or test, thereby minimizing the difficulty for students who read below grade level. Students show what they know without being hindered by their reading disability.

Sticky Note Method of Highlighting

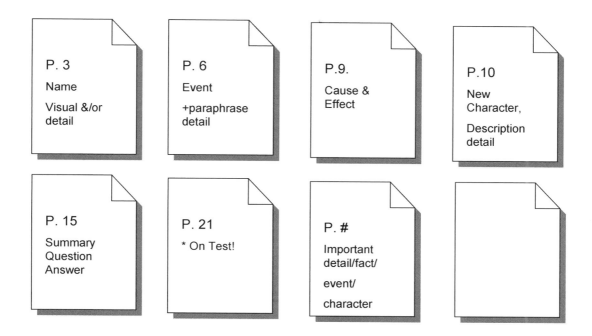

P. 3

Name

Visual &/or detail

P. 6

Event

+paraphrase detail

P.9.

Cause & Effect

P.10

New Character,

Description detail

P. 15

Summary Question Answer

P. 21

* On Test!

P. #

Important detail/fact/

event/

character

As students are reading a text, every time an important fact, item, cause and effect situation, etc., comes up, have students put a post-it note right in that spot and write the page number, the item and a visual or some detail.

After the chapter is read, the novel is finished, or the text section is done, students should take all the sticky notes and line them up sequentially (as in the picture above) on a sheet of 8 ½" X 11" paper.

- Place the paper in a sleeve protector.
- Students now have a study guide that ties into the text.

Paper and Pencil Strategies

- Have students use two colors when working, alternating the color of each fact they are writing in their notes. Color makes facts stand-out as unique. If all notes are in one color, nothing stands out as unique and is therefore harder to remember.
- Highlight important information. Teach what to highlight and what not to highlight. Some students will highlight text randomly.
- Alternate color of bullets using gel pens, markers, crayons, etc.
- When printing, print information in upper and lower case because it makes a clear shape. Printing in all capitals always makes a rectangle. All words then have the same shape which hinders recall.
- Border words in the shape of the word. Even better, color-code the border to categorize parts of speech. For example, nouns bordered in red, verbs in green, pronouns in yellow.

There are patterns in a single printed word. If you take a word and border it, you're making that word – that shape – more visual. There are students who struggle with vocabulary and spelling. But they struggle less with reading if they know the shape of the word. They know what it looks like in their visual memory and when they read a word, they know that if it's not the right shape, it's not the right word.

Many students who learn their vocabulary this way will recognize when a word is not the right shape. This process is a further example of patterns we can use with kids who struggle with vocabulary and reading.

Color-Coded Grammar Poster

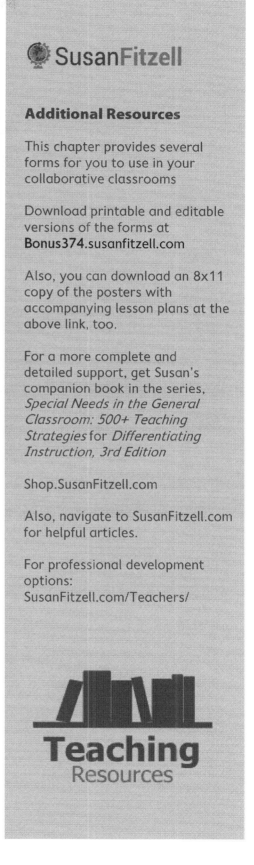

Difficulty/Adaptation Quick List

DIFFICULTY	ADAPTATION
Poor literacy skills	Provide simpler text/use peer support
Speech/language difficulty	Check understanding of key words Partner/group oral work
Listening/following instructions	Highlight/cure in to important information/provide lists
Poor numeric skills	Provide apparatus, e.g. counters, algebra manipulatives
Written work: copying notes, taking notes from lecture, etc.	Use alternative forms of recording
Grasping/retaining new concepts	Give more practice/use smaller steps/use alternative language/use memory strategies
Difficulty with maps/graphs/charts	Tracing photocopy – photocopy and enlarge, add color/shading
Short concentration span/keeping on task	Provide short tasks/frequent verbal cues
Distracts others/is distracted	Sit in front/isolate from others/explore supportive groups
Working independently	Pair with responsible partner
Keeping classroom code of conduct	Give positive reinforcement/diary of specific incidents
Relating to other pupils	Change seating positions or group/monitor triggers
Working in cooperation with others	Pair with responsible partner/define group roles
Relating positively to adults	Be a role model/negotiate one-to-one
Slow paced work	Realistic deadlines/allow extra time
Handwriting/presentation difficulties	Allow extra time and/or alternative ways of recording
Low self-esteem/lack of confidence	Notice positives/plan for success and achievement/give classroom responsibilities
Organizational skills	Encourage use of lists, routines, labels, study buddies
Homework	Time to explain homework in lesson/time for class to record assignment/use parental support
Becoming upset at difficulties	Notice positives/reassure

Chapter 4 Review & Discussion Questions

Understanding Special Needs

This section describes the federally defined terms for specific special needs and learning disabilities, and all related terminology.

Reflect and Discuss

Consider an average school week. How often do you encounter students who require special education services?

What are some of the ways you currently adapt your interactions with these students to ensure they are included in activities without being singled-out?

As mentioned in the "Potential Roadblocks: Differences" section of the chapter, paraprofessionals can often become the sole provider of all teaching and assistance for special education students. After learning about different types of learning disabilities and limitations, has your confidence in your ability to adequately teach and support these students changed? Has it changed for better or worse? Which topic brought about that change?

Learning – How the Brain Learns: Multiple Intelligence &

Setting Up the Environment

This section introduces the idea of multiple modes of learning. The effectiveness of each mode varies depending on the individual's learning preferences.

Reflect and Discuss

1. Which intelligences do you show an affinity for?
2. Which intelligences do you score low on?
3. How have these strengths and weaknesses shaped your approach to teaching?

Take it to the Classroom – Practical Application

Now that you know your strengths, it is time to find out the strengths of your students and try to cater to them.

<u>For teachers</u> - pass out the checklists in this chapter to the students in one of your classes. Analyze the data. How many students do you have in each of the eight intelligences?

Once you have this data, rewrite a future lesson to incorporate the three most populous intelligences, and one or two more instructional approaches if there are any students who do not have a learning preference in the top three.

After you teach the lesson, write a paragraph reflecting on the effect that appealing to these learning preferences had on the following areas: lesson retention, class participation, and individual behavior.

<u>For paraprofessionals</u> - select two to three students you regularly assist and have them complete the checklists in this chapter. Analyze the data – which three instructional approaches do these students prefer the most?

Once you have this data, create, and implement scripts for discussing these new learning insights with all the teachers for those students to convince them to make their lesson appeal to a broader range of learning modalities.

For a teacher that agrees to incorporate supports for these learning preferences into their lessons, try to observe the effects that had on the student in the following areas: lesson retention, class participation, and individual behavior. Write a paragraph describing these effects.

Strategies to Assist with Learning and Approaching Different Assignments

This section introduces a large variety of strategies to assist with learning across assignment types and disciplines that will appeal to different personality types, learning strengths, and suggest ways to offer choice within the same assignment.

If, after completing this section, you find yourself thinking, "There are too many strategies! I feel overwhelmed trying to understand them all," try the following activity.

Strategy Analysis Activity:

If, after completing this section, you find yourself thinking, "*There are too many strategies! I feel overwhelmed trying to understand them all,*" try the following activity.

Instructions:

- ☐ On the lined side of five index cards, draw two lines that cut the card into four equal quadrants.
- ☐ Select five strategies discussed in this chapter. Write each one separately on the unlined side of the index cards.
- ☐ Sort them into groups based on learning preferences. In the top left corner of the lined side, write all the groups that strategy fits within.
- ☐ Now, sort them into groups based on which ones work well for specific special needs and learning disabilities.
- ☐ In the bottom left corner of the lined side, write all of the special needs and disabilities that strategy works well for.
- ☐ On the bottom right side, write all of the special needs and disabilities where that strategy should be avoided.
- ☐ Finally, group the strategies based on which ones would be good alternatives to offer choice. For example, mind mapping as a choice in contrast to teaching each other.
- ☐ On the top right side, write all of the other strategies that could be offered as alternatives to this one.

Each week, you can add a new strategy to your "strategy toolbox."

✥ CHAPTER 5 ☙

Fostering Student Independence

By Guest Author, Janet Hull

Why Increase Student Independence?

To facilitate academic growth and building capacity, schools must appropriately and effectively address the skills needed for students with special needs to expand their levels of independence. Most often, the paraprofessional works closely with school staff and plays an essential and significant role in this process, as the paraprofessional is most often working closely with a student or group of students across a school day, in a variety of structured and un-structured settings. Independence skills will have a positive impact on the quality of life experienced by a student while in school and after completing their public-school education.

Increasing Skills for Independence:

- Increases opportunities for accessing instruction in a less restrictive setting.
- Promotes greater access to same-age non-disabled peers.
- Allows student to practice social skills more frequently across settings.
- Allows students to better manage social situations effectively.
- Bolsters self-esteem in students with special needs.
- Motivates students to achieve, academically and socially.
- Creates an empowered learner despite learning differences.
- Allows staff and student to focus on instruction.
- Increases confidence for asking clarifying questions.
- Provides a "bridge" for bringing two worlds together.
- Supports students with transition into the community and post-graduation opportunities.

Defining Cues and Prompting

A Cue refers to a natural request to follow a direction or engage in a task made by an adult other than the paraprofessional.
Natural Cues in the school setting could include:

- "What do you think you need to do next?"
- "Always capitalize the first word in the sentence."
- Student is given either written directions, visuals, color-coded instructions, to help the student complete a task.

A Prompt refers to any additional information, assistance, and guidance given to the student by the paraprofessional following a natural teacher cue. The prompt would be provided after the student failed to follow a direction after a reasonable wait- time. The additional prompt will increase the likelihood that a student will give an appropriate response

Prompts in the School Setting Could Include:

- Step-by-step instructions are given to a student in order for the student to complete the task.
- Repeated gestures to indicate a place or object or action to indicate the next step of a task.

Using the Prompt Hierarchy

The prompt hierarchy is a systematic method of assisting students in the learning and skill acquisition process. The prompt is used to support students only when needed and only for as long as the student requires them. Most often, the paraprofessional would begin with the least intrusive prompt required to support a student, with an eye on moving to a much less intrusive prompt over time and eventually down to a natural occurring cue in the environment

Least Intrusive to Most:
- Natural teacher cue
- Indirect verbal
- Direct verbal
- Visual/Gesture
- Modeling
- Partial physical
- Full physical

Natural Teacher Cue:

The use of normal, everyday cues that a classroom teacher would use with other students that do not require additional assistance. Natural teacher cues are generally an established part of classroom routines. Keep in mind; it is essential that students be given the opportunity to respond to the natural cues from the teacher prior to receiving an additional prompt from the paraprofessional.

Natural Teacher Cues Could Include:

- Lights on/lights off
- Warm-up on the overhear/blackboard/Smartboard
- Use of schedule book or Agenda
- Class bell
- Announcements
- Peer supports (orchestrated by adult)
- Written schedule on board/ Smartboard

- Picture schedule
- Posted outcomes for the day
- Posted classroom rules
- Hall/bathroom passes
- Prearranged private signals

Indirect Verbal Prompting:

Refers to when an adult asks indirect questions of the student regarding what they need to do to complete a task or activity.

Saying to a student after the initial cue, "What are the steps you need to follow to complete this assignment?" or "What do you need to do next?" or "Where do you think you can find that information?"

Direct Verbal Prompting:

Refers to when an adult provides explicit directions, telling the student specifically what they need to do.

Saying after the initial cue, "You need to pack up the math materials and put them on the shelf." or "Solve problems 3 and 4 on page 16."

Visual/Gestural Prompting:

Refers to pointing or using a gesture (motion) to let the student know what they need to do (pointing, nodding, etc.).

- If a student does not remember to use their hand to anchor a paper before writing; you may point to the area where they have been directed to place their hand on previous occasions.
- An adult could use a gesture or sign language to redirect a student's attention ("look at me".).
- Providing a visual schedule for students to refer to throughout the day.

Modeling:

This is demonstrating a correct response or skill for the student. When the paraprofessional is modeling, verbal prompting may be used as well.

- Demonstrating the proper use of social skills
- Modeling "thinking aloud" while solving a math problem on the Smartboard or demonstrating a science experiment
- Demonstrating how to use a picture schedule appropriately
- Demonstrating how to organize materials for easier access

Partial Physical Prompting:

This type of prompting involves providing a limited amount of physical guidance through a task or activity. This form of prompting will, at times, be paired with verbal or visual prompts.

- Lightly touching the top of a student's hands, nudging them towards an object
- Assisting the student with putting a backpack on or taking it off
- Starting a zipper on a jacket
- Lightly touching your hand to a student's shoulder to redirect them

Full Physical Prompting:

This level of prompting involves using physical contact with the student to guide them through a task or activity.

- Continually guiding the student's hands during hand-washing
- Holding a student's hand as they ascend/descend stairs
- Placing both hands-on the student's shoulder to reposition their body
- Using a 'hand-over-hand' strategy to assist your student with writing tasks. With one hand, show the student how to anchor the paper and, with the other hand, move the student's hand as they go through the motions of writing

Guidelines for Effective Prompting

Remember to:

- Begin with the least intrusive, effective prompt, initially. You can add other prompts if necessary, making the prompt more intrusive, if the student does not respond accurately. This will assist you in avoiding creating a "prompt dependent" student.

- Refrain from providing a prompt for a skill that your student currently performs independently. If a student can carry or retrieve materials on their own, do not assist them with this task.
- Gain student attention before giving a prompt (when needed).
- Avoid over use of verbal prompts when possible.
- Always use prompts in conjunction with some form of verbal or visual reinforcement. Provide positive praise or a small tangible reinforcement for having followed the prompt in a timely manner after it was provided.
- Continue providing reinforcement when the student exhibits the desired behavior/response with a decrease in prompts or without prompting.
- Discontinue using prompts after a student masters a skill.
- Whenever possible, utilize automated prompts (i.e.: bell, timer, etc.) in place of human prompts. Some students may respond to automated prompts more frequently than human prompts and are considered less likely to create prompt dependency over time. An example of this would be using a timer to signal when a student needs to clean-up and put his/her belongings away.
- Work diligently to *fade prompts* as soon as possible to avoid "prompt dependency." For example, if you notice that the student begins to attempt writing without the use of hand-over-hand, do not provide the prompt. If a student responds to a visual prompt by taking out needed materials, do not follow-up with a visual reminder. Additionally, allow for a period of time between the original cue and the follow-up prompt, giving the student an opportunity to respond without a prompt.

Effective Verbal Prompting:

- Providing a verbal prompt could include restating or paraphrasing the original cue from the teacher or it could be as simple as providing a word or phrase. A partial verbal prompt could be as simple as giving the initial sound or syllable of a word.
- Establish eye contact with student prior to giving prompt (when possible).
- Use vocabulary that is familiar to the student.
- Use structurally simple and relatively short sentences when prompting.

- Adjust your rate of speaking when giving a verbal prompt.
- Use "Start" directions in place of "Stop" directions. Let students know what you want them to do, rather than what they should be doing (i.e.: give them the replacement behavior in the verbal prompt).
- Give "wait time" after the prompt. Additionally, allow for a period of time between the original cue and the follow-up prompt, giving the student an opportunity to respond without a prompt.
- Repeat the prompt if needed.

Reinforcing the Response:

- Provide reinforcement for the correct response.
- Give verbal praise to the individual or class.
- Use positive" I" statements: "I like the way you got started quickly."
- Reinforce with sincerity.
- Reinforce with enthusiasm.

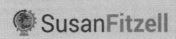

Janet Hull Bio

With over 25 years of experience in education, Janet Hull has been nationally recognized for her work with paraprofessionals. She has taught in high school, middle school and elementary settings and has worked with students with cognitive, behavioral, communication, and autism spectrum disorders. Her vast experience includes working in rural, suburban, urban, and highly diverse schools and school systems. In addition, Janet has been an adjunct professor for many years teaching paraeducators and teachers at the university level. These experiences have led to a deep understanding of the needs and challenges faced by paraeducators.

Fading Prompts Across Settings

Fading Prompts

Allow students to make the shift from responding to additional prompts and to practice responding to natural cues in the instructional environment. Fading is the reduction of the intensity or magnitude of a particular type of prompt over time, while maintaining to provide encouragement and reinforcement.

Prompts can be faded in terms of:
- Intensity
- Location

Fading Prompt Intensity

- Providing a verbal prompt with a decrease in the volume (quietly)
- Saying less of the word (Bob – "B")
- Visual prompts lighter and lighter until they disappear
- Physical prompt tight hand-over-hand reduced to shadowing (without touching the student's hand)
- Reducing the number of prompts given during a period of time

Fading Prompt Location

Full physical hand-over-hand to wrist, to the elbow, to the shoulder, to next to (within one foot), to three feet away, to five feet away, etc.

Proximity to Student:
- Next to student transitioning in halls
- Within line of vision
- Meeting the student at class

Proximity to Student:
- Seated next to student in class
- Moving about the class/going to student only when needed
- Present for only part of class

Proximity to Student:
- Using visual/verbal cues near student
- Using visual cues from other areas of room

Creating the Plan: Fading Adult Support Across Settings

Once the school team has weighed the potential positive and negative outcomes of assigning additional adult support and have reviewed the questions regarding "identified needs" they are ready to develop the plan for "Fading" supports. A plan for "Fading" requires that the team prioritize the student needs, identify the level of prompting anticipated and the criteria by which success will be measured. Providing support using an organized plan will ensure that the student, over time, develops skills of independence.

A plan for "Fading" requires that the team prioritize the student needs, identify the level of prompting anticipated and the criteria by which success will be measured. Providing support using an organized plan will ensure that the student, over time, develops skills of independence.

Monitoring the "Fade Plan":

At the end of each quarter or at the semester break, student progress should be reviewed. Data collected by the paraprofessional would be reported in measurable terms using predetermined checklists or data collection forms. If a student has made measurable progress, then the team would determine the next step towards increasing student independence.

Student Plan for Fading Adult Support

Student: _____ Grade: _____

Area of Need – Transitions
- ☐ Entering school
- ☐ Between classes
- ☐ Within classes
- ☐ Leaving school

Level of Prompt – Prompt Hierarchy
- ☐ Teacher Cue
- ☐ Verbal Indirect
- ☐ Verbal Direct
- ☐ Visual/Gestural
- ☐ Modeling
- ☐ Partial Physical
- ☐ Full Physical

Goal
By _____ student will transition with increased independence
- ☐ Entering school
- ☐ Within school
- ☐ Between activities
- ☐ Leaving School

Outcome: (Student progress during a specified period of time, quarter or semester is recorded. Progress is reported based on the data collected and is reported in measurable terms.)

Thinking it Through
How Much is Too Much and How Much is Too Little?

When a Paraprofessional Provides Support as a 1:1 Aide

Much like the classroom teacher, paraprofessionals make "in the moment" decisions regarding the use of prompting; how intrusive and how frequently it will be utilized.

Questions to Ask When Assessing Student Needs:
1. Is the IEP appropriate? Are there academic goals and objectives that support the development of skills of independence?
2. What specific health, behavior, academic or transition behaviors necessitate the need for additional adult support?
3. Has school staff observed this student across multiple settings?
4. What intervention(s) or program changes have been tried? What was the success?
5. How long were the interventions attempted?
6. What data was collected to assist in the decision-making process?
7. What areas of need have been identified?
   a. Transition
   b. Academic
   c. Behavior
   d. Health/Self-Help

Chapter 5 Review and Discussion Questions

Reflect and Write: Defining Cues and Prompting

List at least three examples of cueing and prompting, besides those listed in the section.

Reflect and Discuss: Using the Prompt Hierarchy and Guidelines for Effective Prompting

- Discuss the hierarchy with your teacher(s) and determine how best to implement prompts in each class and with different students.
- Make a written plan for each class and student.

Reflect and Write: Fading Prompts Across Settings

- Consider the fading techniques outlined in the chapter and determine the prompts appropriate for each student on your case load.
- For each student, make a plan and set goals for fading the prompts required.

Conclusion

Throw the Words, "Just a Paraprofessional" Out the Window

It was during my Paraprofessionals and Teachers Working Together seminar, when a paraprofessional walked up to me and said, "I know that you said we shouldn't ever say, "I'm 'just' a paraprofessional," but, what do I do when my principal says that to me? My principal tells the teacher's assistants at our school we can be replaced. He says we are a dime a dozen."

As I listened to this woman and saw the pain deep in her eyes, I was horrified at the insensitivity and lack of humanity in the words this paraprofessional has heard. How could one human being in our educational community be so incredibly disrespectful to another? Okay, you might be thinking, "Susan, what world do you live in? This often happens in schools." I do know this at some level; I suppose I just don't want to believe it. What could possibly be gained from diminishing the worth of the adults charged with educating and supporting our children?

Is there anything to be gained by creating a culture in our schools where paraprofessionals (teaching assistants, aides, paras, para-pros, classroom assistants) are viewed as 'less than'?

Paraprofessionals have a vital role in our schools. Generally, as one parent expressed, paraprofessionals are the least paid, least trained people in the school community, yet they are often charged with caring for and academically supporting the most challenging and most needy students. Paraprofessionals often work for a salary that is barely above minimum wage. Many are provided with little or no training. They are often excluded from staff development opportunities or are only invited to participate without compensation.

Imagine the chaos in our cafeterias, the pandemonium on the playground, the commotion in the classroom if not for the supervision of paraprofessionals. Paraprofessionals are critical to providing the best supportive educational environment for students.

Paraprofessionals, like teachers, come into the educational system with diverse backgrounds and abilities. Teachers and administrators need to tap into a paraprofessional's strengths. When we work together to maximize a

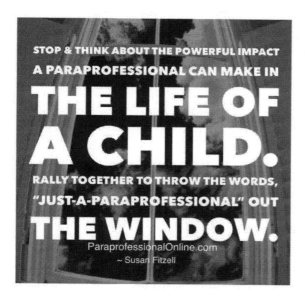

STOP & THINK ABOUT THE POWERFUL IMPACT
A PARAPROFESSIONAL CAN MAKE IN
THE LIFE OF A CHILD.
RALLY TOGETHER TO THROW THE WORDS,
"JUST-A-PARAPROFESSIONAL" OUT
THE WINDOW.
ParaprofessionalOnline.com
~ Susan Fitzell

paraprofessional's talents and empower them to use those talents in our schools, we all benefit, especially the children. Read on for some powerful testimonials that give credence to the value of our paraprofessionals.

Carol Ekster, a recently retired teacher in New Hampshire expressed her appreciation for her paraprofessional, Karen. She wrote, "Susan, I taught in Derry, New Hampshire for 35 years. Last year was my last year teaching and I had a one-on-one aide in my room for a William's Syndrome child. She was dedicated to that child's welfare, rarely absent, thoughtful, and loving to other children who benefited from her attention, and always willing to help me if needed. She thought about that child and the class at home, bringing in relevant or needed things at her own expense. She was one of those humble and incredibly giving people who made a difference in our classroom last year."

Is there a human being dedicated to the welfare of our children that could sleep at night if they considered Karen, "just" a paraprofessional? I hope not. Julia Hornberger, a special education teacher at Muhlenberg High School in Pennsylvania adds, "For the last five years, I have had the great pleasure of working with Kathy Etchberger. During a transition period between paraprofessionals for my caseload, Kathy was hired as a substitute. I admired her immediately, as she was confident, competent, and caring. It was the first time in my career that someone besides my wonderful mentor was actually helping me, and the students absolutely loved her. Unfortunately, Kathy was not hired as my full-time paraprofessional. I was devastated. She was everything that I needed in a paraprofessional and, even more, as a friend."

Julia continues, "Luckily for both of us, she was later hired as the paraprofessional for my mentor teacher. Even though she isn't "assigned" to my caseload anymore, she is literally right next door. Kathy knows what I need, often before I even know that I need it, and she is always there to help and guide me. I like to consider her the "rock star" of my close group of teaching friends. Any time I am in the hallway with her, students are always calling her out and coming to share good news with her - something which never ceases to amaze me. She has such a positive impact on everyone who surrounds her. Kathy has truly touched my life, and I am so grateful for all that she has given me"

Michael Tinker, from W. G. Vinal Elementary School in Massachusetts shares this story about a crowded cafeteria, a baloney sandwich, and a very astute, quick thinking paraprofessional. "A boy was choking on a baloney sandwich in the cafeteria. The chaos and decibel level was tipping into the red on the meter, yet one of our paraprofessionals, Sue Scott, picked him out - even though this child was in the middle of everyone and everything. Because of her quick thinking, the child was okay. Then, last year, we lost one of our colleagues, a kindergarten teacher. Sue was close to the teacher who passed away yet, rather than grieve, she went in "for the kids" until the school could find another teacher. She helped give the kindergarteners the stability they needed by being the long-term substitute. In both situations, Sue made a huge difference. She was there first and foremost for the kids. She quite literally saved the day."

Teachers are not the only ones who appreciate their paraprofessionals. Often, parents are deeply impacted by the quality of care their children receive from paraprofessionals.

STOP & THINK ABOUT THE POWERFUL IMPACT

A PARAPROFESSIONAL CAN MAKE IN THE LIFE OF A CHILD. RALLY TOGETHER TO THROW THE WORDS, "JUST-A-PARAPROFESSIONAL" OUT THE WINDOW.
~ Susan Fitzell

Heidi Crum of Denver, Colorado shares a parent's perspective. Her son, Cal, has cerebral palsy and needs a one-on-one assistant. Her son has that and more in Erin. Erin has been working with Cal for the past two years. Heidi explains that she's an outstanding para. She works to create a lot of independence for him. He makes progress, and may flatten out for a while, then grows again. This concerned mom understands the struggles paraprofessionals face. She notes that paras must know when to push and when not to, in order to promote self-sufficiency in their students. This is not always black and white and is a continual dilemma for the paraprofessional. Heidi appreciates that Erin is willing to discuss Cal's progress calmly and professionally. She works as a team with the teachers and makes sure that other paras work with Cal so he's not dependent on her. She truly takes ownership of her work.

Heidi believes strongly that it is very important for teachers and paraprofessionals to be a team. From a parent's point of view, the paraprofessional becomes the frontline person. She explains, "She's the one primarily interacting with, and developing, my child as a learner. There is so much interaction between the child and para. It impacts how the child views himself and his abilities." It's very important for the teachers and paras to work together for the benefit of the child.

I remember Jay Gratton from teaching high school. Jay would walk into my class and his smile would light up the room. Jay learned differently. I recently heard Jay speak at the retirement party of an amazing human being, a paraprofessional, Kathy Wicker, who meant so incredibly much to many, but also to Jay and I. Jay shared these words from the podium, "I am a special education teacher at Merrimack High School. Not only am I an alumnus of Londonderry High School and their Special Ed. Department, but I was also lucky enough to work at Londonderry High School for 3 years as a para. I have never been around someone who gives more of them self than Mrs. Wicker. Her tremendous dedication to her family, colleagues, friends, and students is inspiring. For me, Mrs. Wicker took a student who doubted his every ability and who wanted nothing to do with school and turned him into a four-year honor student in one quarter. Mrs. Wicker was an angel that never left my side in high school and never let me fall. When I would stumble she would always be there to help me up. It is very simple; I loved this woman and still do very, very much." Jay spoke these words directly to Kathy, "The main reason I went into education is because of you, Mrs. Wicker. I can't even imagine where I would be right now without you being involved in my life. If I can make just half the impact on one student that you made on me, then I will have been a success. If I can make just one student feel as special and as important as you made me feel, then I will have been a success. At school, I am constantly asking myself what you would do in a given situation and that is the reason your compassion, heart, enthusiasm and love for helping others will always have a place in New Hampshire schools."

What Jay doesn't know is that Kathy was also a formative role model for me. Kathy taught me the importance of appreciating my colleagues. She always knew when someone needed a pat on the back, a hug, or a Snickers bar. I learned to be a better colleague from her.

Jodi Roberts, a paraprofessional in Surprise, Arizona tells us, "Several years ago, there was an instructional coach, April, in the district who would observe classes and coach teachers. She would then leave the teachers little sticky notes with suggestions. One day while I was talking to April I must have said five times, "Well, I'm just a T.A. (Teacher's Assistant). I used to say that all the time. I felt unworthy. I have a college degree and have spent years working in schools, but I still lacked confidence. One day, after a conversation with April, I found a sticky note from her that said, "You are not "just" a T.A." I saved that forever and always remembered that." Jodi explains, "Words are powerful."

I sincerely believe that most paraprofessionals are valued by the teachers with whom they work. I believe that most administrators understand and appreciate the contribution that paraprofessionals make in their schools. I believe that if we simply stop and think about the powerful impact a paraprofessional can make in the life of a child, we can rally together to "Throw the words, "just a paraprofessional" out the window."

Are you with me? Pass this one to your education colleagues and join the campaign to appreciate the contribution of paraprofessionals in your school.

Online Resources

American Federation of Teachers Paraprofessional and School-Related Personnel
Web site www.aft.org/psrp/

Minnesota Paraprofessional Consortium
University of Minnesota
111 Pattee Hall; 150 Pillsbury Drive SE
Minneapolis, MN 55455
612-624-9893
Web site: http://ici2.umn.edu/para/

National Resource Center for Paraprofessionals in Education and Related Services
Utah State University
Logan, UT 84322-6526
435-797-7272
Web site: http://www.nrcpara.org

The PAR²A Center
University of Colorado at Denver
Contact: Dr. Nancy French, Director
Web site: http://paracenter.org/

The Center provides the Paraeducator Supervision Academy, comprehensive curriculum packages for paraeducators serving English Language Learners, students with low-incidence disabilities, and many more professional development opportunities.

Paraeducator.com*
Web site: http://www.paraeducator.com/

A resource for paraeducators in Washington state. Includes training modules in the core competencies for paraeducators, online discussion groups, and fact sheets concerning new Title I requirements.
*This site does not appear to have been updated since 2010. That said, there's still some valuable information on the site, so I'm including it.

ParaEducate.com
Website:
http://www.paraeducate.com/
Twitter:

https://twitter.com/Paraeducate
Facebook:
https://www.facebook.com/ParaEducate/

ParaEducate: Resources for Special Education
Since 2012, ParaEducate has been a resource for special education teachers, paraeducators, and act as advocates for people with disabilities. We have provided a variety of information through our books, blog, and conferences. Find out more about ParaEducate.

How to Facilitate a Book Study

Individual Book Study

This book is designed to serve as both a functional reference as well as a textbook that can be used as part of a formal course, individual book study, or guided group study.

Completing the book study as an individual is a simple process:

Read each chapter.

Consider the Chapter Review/Discussion Questions and jot down or record your reflections.

NOTE: If you intend to obtain a Verification of Completion for this course, you may need to provide copies of your responses to these questions.

Implement techniques and strategies in your day-to-day classroom teaching process as outlined (Required for graduate credit).

Group Oriented Book Study

We encourage you to complete this book study as part of a community of learners, where possible:

- Department or grade level teams.
- Core academic teams.
- Vertical teams (across grade level), by subject area.
- Any other reasonable grouping technique that works for your campus or activity.

1. Each group will need a group facilitator or team leader.
2. Determine your groups or teams.
3. Clearly outline a timeline of reading goals.
4. Set dates and times to meet for group discussion of Review/Discussion Questions and application of strategy ideas.
5. Establish ground rules. Use the section in the book on setting ground rules for students as an action learning activity for the group. Simply adjust the activity for adult learners.

Tips for Being a Good Facilitator

- Create a relaxed atmosphere for the group.
- Treat everyone with respect.
- Consider having a co-facilitator, especially for larger groups.

Remember that the term "facilitator" means "to make easy." Your job is to make it easy for everyone to participate. This will help participants feel comfortable and foster an atmosphere of helpful cooperation for everyone, including you.

Be prepared – Understand the Chapter Review/Discussion questions. The facilitator is responsible for keeping the discussion on target and allowing everyone to have a voice in discussion.

First Meeting

- Be sure all group members have a book.
- Have all group members introduce themselves, if necessary.
- Be sure everyone understands the purpose and goals of the study.
- Review the course requirements, proposed timeline, and meeting schedule.

All Meetings

- Ask group members to bring their books and notes to every meeting.
- A good way to start is to review the Review/Discussion questions and go over the pages of the book that may apply to the questions.
- The goal of group meetings is to be sure that all members have completed the chapter exercises, promote discussion, and foster an environment of mutual motivation and cooperation.

Review/Discussion Questions and this Guide

- If conversation wanders from the topic, return to the discussion questions, but remember that good discussion is sometimes more important than covering all the questions.
- Try to involve everyone.

Leading Discussions

- Pose one question, or scenario, at a time to the group.
- Pre-select the questions or scenarios to discuss, based on group and school needs. Write each on an index card and pass them out to the group members. Each participant (or team of two or three) takes a card and addresses the question or scenario on their card.
- Have participants model strategies discussed in the reading to address questions or scenarios (Mind maps, mnemonics, snapshot devices, etc.)

Group Discussions Without a Facilitator

If the group facilitator is unable to attend and no alternate has been designated, continue with the meeting and discussion without them.

- Take turns going around the room, allowing each group member to talk about his or her experience or reflections on the reading. Set a time limit for discussion of each participant's comments.
- Hand out index cards. Ask everyone to write a question or observation; then select one or more to discuss. Set time limits for discussion of each card.

Book Study Activities

Fishbowl Activity

The fishbowl exercise allows the facilitator to demonstrate how a book study works, and what good facilitation looks like.

Ask for a few volunteers (6 to 8 max) and seat them in a circle with an experienced facilitator inside the "fishbowl." (You can facilitate this group, or have another skilled facilitator do it.) The other participants can sit or stand around the small group to observe. The facilitator begins by welcoming everyone, initiating introductions, and explaining the impartial role of the facilitator.

The facilitator will help the group set its ground rules. Then the discussion begins and continues for several minutes. During the discussion, the facilitator should introduce some typical opening session questions such as personal concerns about the issue, as well as some questions that help people consider different viewpoints on the issue (typical of later study circle sessions). During the fishbowl, the facilitator should demonstrate some paraphrasing, clarifying, summarizing, or other common facilitation techniques. Involve the entire group in debriefing the exercise, using the questions below.

Post these questions where everyone can see them in the debriefing demonstration after the fishbowl activity.

What did the facilitator do to:
- set a positive tone?
- explain and help the group set the ground rules?
- help people connect their concerns and values to the issue?
- manage the discussion process? For example, what interventions did he or she use?
- help advance the group's understanding of the content?
- make sure that different views were considered?
- bring out some of the complexities of the issue?
- try to involve everyone in the discussion?
Were those techniques effective? Would another approach have been better?

Search-Pair-Share

Purpose: To increase the amount of information sharing from a search.

Time	Facilitator Activities	Participant Activities	Techniques & Equipment
30 min	Provide information on *<insert topic>* for research	Identify reference material for *<insert topic>*	Pairs, text, flip chart paper, markers.
10 min	Collect and comment on sources and debrief activity	List sources Discuss aids to process	Whole group

Activity Explanation and Instructions:

Facilitator: When an activity to address a specific standard is needed that also meets the needs of all learners, it may be difficult to locate one. It is easier when material has been previewed, and references are organized in advance.

Objective: Identify the topic to be addressed: *<insert topic>* and create a list of suggestions from the text to address that issue or topic while meeting the needs of different participants.

Techniques/Equipment: Written text materials, flipcharts, and markers, etc. Monitor and encourage participation.

Process: In pairs:
- Find as many activities, ideas, etc. to effectively address *<insert topic>* in the text within the next [10] minutes.
- Summarize the activity/idea and main points.

Group Success: All participants can explain the main points.
Accountability: Pairs share their references and information with the whole group. A combined list of references is created.
Debrief: What were the differences that you saw in how your pair and other pairs searched for references? How did this affect the length of the compiled list?

Pair, Read, Respond

Purpose: To increase comprehension by using shared readings.

Time	Facilitator Activities	Participant Activities	Techniques & Equipment
25 min	Provide section/chapter information on reading & guide activity	Describe information on *<insert topic>*	Pairs, written information
10 min	Ensure comprehension Debrief activity	Answer content questions Discuss group process	Whole group

Activity Explanation and Instructions:

Objective: Describe *<insert content>*

Time: 35 minutes (5 min set up, 2x10 for pair reading, 10 min debrief)

Techniques/Equipment: One copy of *<insert content>* information to each person. Monitor and encourage participation.

Process: Individually — Silently read each paragraph or section and then, in pairs:

- Take turns describing the content of the reading to their partner. Discrepancies in understanding are discussed as needed.
- When each pair finishes, they might discuss the entire passage.

Group Success: Both people in the group can describe the passage content.
Accountability: Randomly answer questions on content.
Debrief: Was this an effective means of covering this material for you? Why or why not?

What Worries You?

Purpose: To bring out fears so that they can be addressed and handled. Change is difficult. So much is at stake for teachers in today's classrooms that, sometimes, putting those fears out "on the table" for discussion is the best way to address them.

Time	Facilitator Activities	Learner Activities	Techniques & Equipment
10 min	Pose *<insert topic area>* and ask for "nightmares" Guide activity	Identify the worst case scenarios that you can imagine for *<insert topic>*	Pairs, 5x7 cards, markers or felt pens
10 min	Collect cards for reference Debrief activity	Discuss scenarios and perceptions	Whole group

Activity Explanation and Instructions:

Facilitator: What we don't know how to deal with may make us quite nervous.

Objective: Identify imaginary but realistic worst-case scenarios for *<insert topic>* situations.

Time: 20 minutes

Techniques/Equipment: Large sticky notes or 5x7 cards, colored markers or felt pens.

Process:
- Individually – Each participant writes out a <insert topic> scenario that they dread (real or imagined).
- In pairs – Discuss the worst case for each scenario.

Group Success: Both participants can identify with the feelings of the other.
Accountability: Scenarios are described to the whole group. Group posts scenarios for review.
Debrief: How does discussing "worst case scenarios" change your perception of what might happen and what you might do about it?

Bibliography

Alivisatos, A. P., Chun, M., Church, G. M., Greenspan, R. J., Roukes, M. L., & Yuste, R. (2012). The brain activity map project and the challenge of functional connectomics. *Neuron, 74*(6), 970–4. http://doi.org/10.1016/j.neuron.2012.06.006

Austin, S. F. (2012). *The effects of professional development for the Alt-MSA: Impact on classroom instruction. Dissertation Abstracts International Section A: Humanities and Social Sciences.*

Brock, M. E., & Carter, E. W. (2013). A systematic review of paraprofessional-delivered educational practices to improve outcomes for students with intellectual and developmental disabilities. *Research and Practice for Persons with Severe Disabilities, 38*. http://doi.org/10.1177/154079691303800401

Caine, R. N., Caine, G., McClintic, C., Klimek, K. J., & Costa, A. L. (n.d.). *12 brain/mind learning principles in action : teach for the development of higher-order thinking and executive function.*

Chansky, T. E. (2000). *Freeing Your Child from Obsessive-Compulsive Disorder: Step by Step Guidelines* (1st ed.). New York, N.Y.: Three Rivers Press.

Claussen M.H., D., Thaut, Claussen, D., Thaut, M., & Claussen; Thaut; (1997). Music as a Mnemonic Device for Children with Learning Disabilities. *Canadian Journal of Music Therapy, 5*, 55–66.

Conderman, G., & Hedin, L. R. (2015). Using Cue Cards in Inclusive Middle School Classrooms. *The Clearing House: A Journal of Educational Strategies, Issues and Ideas, 88*(5), 155–160. http://doi.org/10.1080/00098655.2015.1061971

Cooper, K. J. (1999, November 26). Study Says Natural Classroom Lighting Can Aid Achievement. *The Washington Post.*

Cowan, N. (2001). The magical number 4 in short-term memory: a reconsideration of mental storage capacity. *The Behavioral and Brain Sciences, 24*(1), 87-114–85.

Cowan, N. (2010). The Magical Mystery Four: How is Working Memory Capacity Limited, and Why? *Current Directions in Psychological Science a Journal of the American Psychological Society, 19*(1), 51–57. http://doi.org/10.1177/0963721409359277

Farrington, J. (2011). Seven plus or minus two. *Performance Improvement Quarterly, 23*(4), 113–116. http://doi.org/10.1002/piq.20099

Fitzell, S. G. (2007). *Transforming anger to personal power : an anger management curriculum for grades 6-12. Transforming anger to personal power: An anger management curriculum for Grades 6-12.* Champaign: Research Press.

Gfeller, K. E. (1983). Musical Mnemonics as an Aid to Retention with Normal and Learning Disabled Students. *Journal of Music Therapy, 20,* 179–189.

Giangreco, M. F., Edelman, S. W., & Broer, S. M. (2001). Respect, Appreciation, and Acknowledgment of Paraprofessionals Who Support Students with Disabilities. *Exceptional Children, 67*(4), 485–498.

Giangreco, M. F., Edelman, S. W., Luiselli, T. E., & Macfarland, S. Z. C. (1997). Helping or Hovering? Effects of Instructional Assistant Proximity on Students with Disabilities. *Exceptional Children, 64*(1), 7–18.

Gordon, R., & Gordon, M. (2006). *The Turned-off Child: Learned Helplessness and School Failure.* Salt Lake City, UT: Millennial Mind Publishing.

Hall, R. H., & Sidio-Hall, M. A. (1994). The Effect of Student Color Coding of Knowledge Maps and Test Anxiety on Student Learning. *The Journal of Experimental Education, 62*(4), 291–302. http://doi.org/10.1080/00220973.1994.9944136

Hayes, B. K., Heit, E., & Rotello, C. M. (2014). Memory, Reasoning, and Categorization: Parallels and Common Mechanisms. *Frontiers in Psychology, 5*(JUN), 1–9. http://doi.org/10.3389/fpsyg.2014.00529

Hughes, L., & Wilkins, A. (2000). Large Print and Reading Independence. *Journal of Research in Reading.*

Jausovec, N., Jausovec, K., & Gerlic, I. (2006). The influence of Mozart's music on brain activity in the process of learning. *Clinical Neurophysiology : Official Journal of the International Federation of Clinical Neurophysiology, 117*(12), 2703–2714. http://doi.org/10.1016/j.clinph.2006.08.010

Kelly, P. E. (1977). *Guidelines for the Training, Utilization, and Supervision of Paraprofessionals and Aides [microform] / Phyllis E. Kelly and Others.* (T. Kansas State Dept. of Education, Ed.). [Washington, D.C.]: Distributed by ERIC Clearinghouse.

Kohn, A. (1993). Choices for Children: Why and How to Let Students Decide. *Phi Delta Kappan, 75*(1), 8–16,18–21 Sep 1993.

Kriegeskorte, N., Goebel, R., & Bandettini, P. (2006). Information-based functional brain mapping. *Proceedings of the National Academy of Sciences of the United States of America, 103*(10), 3863–8. http://doi.org/10.1073/pnas.0600244103

Marzano, R. J. (2010). The Art and Science of Teaching/Representing Knowledge Nonlinguistically. *Educational Leadership, 67*(8), 84–86.

Mastropieri, M. A., & Scruggs, T. E. (1998). Enhancing School Success with Mnemonic Strategies. *Intervention in School and Clinic.* http://doi.org/10.1177/105345129803300402

McDonnell, J. (1987). The effects of time delay and increasing prompt hierarchy strategies on the acquisition of purchasing skills by students with severe handicaps. *Journal of the Association for Persons with*

Severe Handicaps., *12*, 227–236.

McVay, P. (1998). Paraprofessionals in the classroom: What role do they play? *Disability Solutions*, *3*(1), 2–4.

Oberauer, K., & Hein, L. (2012). Attention to Information in Working Memory. *Current Directions in Psychological Science*, *21*(3), 164–169. http://doi.org/10.1177/0963721412444727

Oei, N. Y. L., Everaerd, W. T. A. M., Elzinga, B. M., Van Well, S., & Bermond, B. (2006). Psychosocial stress impairs working memory at high loads: An association with cortisol levels and memory retrieval. *Stress (Amsterdam, Netherlands)*, *9*(3), 133–141. http://doi.org/10.1080/10253890600965773

Org, N., Caine, R. N., & Caine, G. (n.d.). The 12 Brain/Mind Natural Learning Principles Expanded 12 Brain/Mind Natural Learning Principles.

Rogers, J. J. (n.d.). The Council for Disability Rights. Retrieved April 23, 2017, from http://www.disabilityrights.org/glossary.htm

Romain, T., & Verdick, E. (2000). *Stress can really get on your nerves!* Minneapolis: Free Spirit Publications.

Rowe, M. B. (1986). Wait Time: Slowing Down May Be A Way of Speeding Up! *Journal of Teacher Education*, *37*(1), 43–50. http://doi.org/10.1177/002248718603700110

Russel, C. (2010). *Effects of decreasing paraprofessional interactions on task engagement in an inclusive classroom*. Oklahoma State University.

Salmelin, R., & Baillet, S. (2009). Electromagnetic brain imaging. *Human Brain Mapping*, *30*(6), 1753–7. http://doi.org/10.1002/hbm.20795

U.S. Department of Education. (2017). Individuals with Disabilities Education Act. Retrieved April 23, 2017, from https://www2.ed.gov/about/offices/list/osers/osep/osep-idea.html

Vedhara, K., Hyde, J., Gilchrist, I. D., Tytherleigh, M., & Plummer, S. (2000). Acute stress, memory, attention and cortisol. *Psychoneuroendocrinology*, *25*(6), 535–549. http://doi.org/10.1016/S0306-4530(00)00008-1

Wallace, W. T. (1994). Memory for music: Effect of melody on recall of text. *Journal of Experimental Psychology: Learning, Memory, Cognition*, *20*, 1471–1485.

Wong, B. (2011). Points of view: Layout. *Nature Methods*, *8*(10), 783–783. http://doi.org/10.1038/nmeth.1711

any sources cited here, nor do we take responsibility for any changes to information or web sites that may occur after verification. If you find an error or would like to alert us to a change to any resource cited herein, please contact us online: http://susanfitzell.com/contact-susan-fitzell/

Appendix

NOTES

_____

_____

_____

_____

_____

_____

_____

_____

_____

_____

_____

_____

_____

_____

_____

_____

_____

_____

_____

_____

_____

NOTES

NOTES

NOTES

Bring Susan to Your School for Consultation or In-Service

Susan Fitzell, M.Ed., CSP, has nearly 25 years of expertise as a teacher, educational consultant, and leadership coach. She is a sought-after speaker, educating and inspiring thousands each year and is the author of over a dozen books on collaborative teaching, ed-tech, learning strategies, & inclusion.

Susan's keynotes and workshops are interactive, content rich, dynamic presentations. She customizes to meet her clients' needs to ensure relevance to the client organizations' dynamics.

Choose from four customizable topics:

Motivating Students to Choose Success
Learn practical strategies to motivate your students to make positive choices, put forth their best effort, & realize they are in control of their own destiny.

Co-teaching & Collaboration for All
Maximize the skills of co-teachers & specialists in your inclusive classrooms with NEW, concrete implementation approaches that take the guesswork out of collaboration.

Differentiation Strategy Blast
Discover a variety of brain-based, research supported, "implement tomorrow" strategies that maintain rigor, maximize time, and increase success for all learners.

Paraprofessionals and Teachers Working Together
Four mini-workshops in one day to strengthen critical skills needed for success in the classroom.: 1. Build a Strong Foundation for Success, 2. How to Collaborate Successfully, 3. Positive Behavior Management and 4. Academic Support

Launch your conference or benefit with Susan's Keynote:
Differentiated Instruction: Why Bother? Aka: Inclusion: Why Bother?
Shift mind-sets that challenge successful differentiated instruction and

inclusive practices. The motto of this powerful keynote is "Good for all, critical for the students with special needs."

**Enhance your Learning Communities with
Our Professional Development Kits
Outstanding Options to Fit any Budget!**

The Standard Multi-User Professional Development Kit:
Choose your topic:

- *Special Needs in the General Classroom, 500 + Teaching Strategies for Differentiating Instruction*
- *Co-Teaching and Collaboration in the Classroom*
- *Paraprofessionals and Teachers Working Together*

You'll Receive:
- A book for each program participant including instructions for the facilitator and study questions.
- Video examples of key strategies and techniques
- Downloadable versions of key forms and handouts
- Complimentary subscription to Susan Fitzell's Tips and Tools newsletter
- A Certification of completion for every participant who submits required criteria
- PowerPoint slides packaged to support key points of discussion

**$159.95/year for district set-up fee plus $19.95 per person
(minimum 50 participants)**

**To Order
Call us at 603-625-6087 or
Email sfitzell@SusanFitzell.com
For more information:**
susanfitzell.com/pd-differentiated-instruction

*Prices subject to change as of 2018

**Enhance your Learning Communities with
Our Professional Development Kits
Outstanding Options to Fit any Budget!**

The Custom Site-Based Professional Development Kit:
Choose your topic:

- *Special Needs in the General Classroom, 500 + Teaching Strategies for Differentiating Instruction*
- *Co-Teaching and Collaboration in the Classroom*
- *Paraprofessionals and Teachers Working Together*

You'll Receive:
- *Everything included in the Standard Multi-User Professional Development Kit
- One hour phone consultation with Susan Fitzell to discuss customizations
- Three hours of video or teleconference coaching with Susan Fitzell and participating staff

**$1995.95 plus $19.95 per person
(minimum participants not required)**

**To Order
Call us at 603-625-6087 or
Email sfitzell@SusanFitzell.com
For more information:**
susanfitzell.com/pd-differentiated-instruction

*Prices subject to change as of 2018

Bring Instructional Strategies or Co-teaching UP a Level with Coaching Support

Coaching Session Options

Option One: Coaching Session

1. Individual teacher identifies concerns and best possible outcome.
2. Teacher requests consultant to
   - Observe X, Y, or Z within the classroom.
   - Suggest strategies and techniques to address concerns.
3. Set up follow-up time
4. Consultant & teacher discuss options available to address concerns.
5. Teacher implements new strategies.
6. Consultant follows up with teacher to provide ongoing support.

Option Two: Materials Adaptation

1. Teacher comes to session with lesson plan and all materials required to implement the lesson.
2. Consultant works with the teacher to identify and where possible prepare simple adaptations to meet student Individual Education Plan needs.

Option Three: Co-planning: Chunking Lesson Plans™

1. Co-teachers come to session with lesson plan goals and all materials required to plan the lesson.
2. Consultant works with co-teachers to plan together taking into consideration professional roles in the classroom as well as multiple ability levels. Co-teachers are encouraged and coached to contribute "both" their ideas for creating or enhancing a lesson plan.

   NOTE: *Coaching sessions are NON-EVALUATIVE. Confidentiality is always maintained.*

**IF YOU DIDN'T DO IT YET, DON'T FORGET
GET YOUR BONUS RESOURCES HERE:**
http://Bonus374.susanfitzell.com

DID YOU FIND A TYPO?

Although this document has been thoroughly reviewed and edited, there is always a chance that we missed something. If you find a typo or other issue in this book, send it to me in email at sfitzell@susanfitzell.com and you will be entered into our monthly prize drawing!

School Professional Development License Agreement

This AimHi Educational Programs, LLC license agreement is subject to change without notice. It is the user's responsibility to check the license agreement prior to conducting training.

The licensing agreement can be found here:

license.susanfitzell.com